Mr. Chimp
& Other Plays

PUBLICATIONS OF THE NORTH AMERICAN JULES VERNE SOCIETY

The Palik Series (edited by Brian Taves)

The Marrriage of a Marquis (*The Marriage of Mr. Anselme des Tilleuls* and *Jédédias Jamet, or The Tale of an Inheritance*)
   Contributors: Edward Baxter, Jean-Michel Margot, Walter James Miller, Kieran M. O'Driscoll, Brian Taves

Shipwrecked Family: Marooned with Uncle Robinson
   Translated by Sidney Kravitz

The Count of Chanteleine: A Tale of the French Revolution
   Translated by Edward Baxter; Notes by Garmt de Vries-Uiterweed, Volker Dehs

Stories by Jules and Michel Verne (*Fact-Finding Mission, Pierre-Jean*, and *The Fate of Jean Morénas*)
   Translated, with notes, by Kieran M. O'Driscoll

Historical Novels: *San Carlos* and *The Siege of Rome*
   Translated by Edward Baxter

(Other volumes in preparation)

The North American Jules Verne Society also copublished (with Prometheus)

Journey Through the Impossible
   Translated by Edward Baxter; Notes by Jean-Michel Margot

Editorial Committee of the North American Jules Verne Society:

Henry G. Franke III   Dr. Terry Harpold
Jean-Michel Margot   Dr. Brian Taves

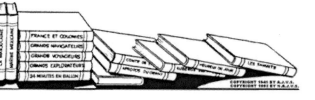

Mr. Chimp & Other Plays

by Jules Verne

Translated by Frank Morlock

Introduction by Jean-Michel Margot

Edited, with notes, by Brian Taves
for the
North American Jules Verne Society

The Palik Series

BearManor Fiction
2011

Mr. Chimp & Other Plays
by Jules Verne

Translations and adaptations of the plays © 2003 by Frank Morlock

Introduction © 2011 by Jean-Michel Margot

Critical material © 2010 by the North American Jules Verne Society

For information, address:

BearManor Fiction
P. O. Box 71426
Albany, GA 31708

bearmanormedia.com

North American Jules Verne Society: najvs.org

Typesetting and layout by John Teehan

Cover design by John Teehan

Back cover from an 1881 poster for the American stage production of the Verne/ D'Ennery *Michael Strogoff*, presented by Kiralfy Bros.

Published in the USA by BearManor Media

ISBN—1-59393-363-0
978-1-59393-363-0

Table of Contents

In memory of

Zvi Har'El

*Who did so much to promote the global union
of Verne enthusiasts*

Jules Verne's Own Reflections

Throughout Jules Verne's life, as he became an ever more legendary author, he accepted requests for meetings with journalists from many nations. Such interviews continued as the author aged, until just before his death in 1905 at age 77. They provide the only lengthy sources, in any language, where Verne offers this type of autobiography.

"When did your career as an author begin?"

"That is a question which will permit of a double answer," he replied. "As early as twelve or fourteen I was never without a pen in my hand, and during my school days I was always writing, my tasks being chiefly poetical. During the whole of my life I have always had a great passion for poetical and dramatic work, and in my later youth I published a considerable number of pieces, some of which met with a fair amount of success.

"I cannot remember the time when I did not write, or intend to be an author; and as you will soon see, many things conspired to that end. I began to write at the age of twelve. It was all poetry then, and dreadful poetry, too. Still, I remember that an address which I composed for my father's birthday—what we call a 'compliment' in France—was thought very good, and I was so complimented that I felt quite proud. I remember that even at that time I used to spend a long time over my writings, copying and correcting, and never really satisfied with what I had done.

"I was educated at the Lycée of Nantes, where I remained till I had finished my rhetoric classes, when I was sent to Paris to study law. As a student in Brittany, I perpetrated half a dozen tragedies, or, in other words, wrote them and then being possessed with the idea that I was a budding young genius, for whose talents Brittany offered too little scope, I packed my valise and started for Paris. My favorite study had always been geography, but at the time that I went to Paris I was entirely taken up with literary projects.

"I came to Paris as a student just about the time when the grisette and all that she meant was disappearing from the Latin quarter. I cannot say that I frequented many of my fellow-students' rooms, for we Britons, you know, are a clannish people, and nearly all my friends were schoolmates from Nantes, who had come up to the Paris University with me. My friends were nearly all musicians, and at that period of my life I was a musician myself. I understood harmony, and I think that I may say that, if I had taken to a musical career, I should have had less difficulty than many in succeeding. Victor Masse was a friend of mine as a student, and so was Delibes, with whom I was very intimate. We used to say 'thou' to each other.

"Amongst my Breton friends was Aristide Hignard, a musician, who, although he won a second Prix de Rome, never emerged from the crowd. We used to collaborate together. I wrote the words and he the music. We produced one or two operettes which were played, and some songs.

"One of these songs, entitled 'Les Gabiers,' which used to be sung by the baritone Charles Patellae, was very popular at the time. The chorus, I remember, was:

> 'Alerte,
> Alerte, enfants, alerte,
> Le ciel est blue, la mer est verte,
> Alerte, alerte.'"

"I was greatly under the influence of Victor Hugo, indeed, very excited by reading and re-reading his works. At that time I could have recited by heart whole pages of *Notre-Dame de Paris* (*The Hunchback of Notre-Dame*, 1831), but it was his dramatic work that most influenced me, and it was under this influence that, at the age of seventeen, I wrote a number of tragedies and comedies, not to mention novels. Thus, I wrote a five-act tragedy in verse, entitled *Alexandre VI*, which was the tragedy of the Borgia pope. Another five-act tragedy in verse, written at that time, was *La Conspiration des poudres* (*The Gunpowder Plot*), with Guy Fawkes as hero. *Un Drame sous Louis XV* (*A Drama Under Louis XV*) was another tragedy in verse, and for comedy there was one in five acts and verse called *Les Heureux du jour* (*Happy for One Day*). All this work was done with the greatest care and with a constant preoccupation after style before me.

"But the friend to whom I owe the deepest debt of gratitude and affection is Alexandre Dumas the younger, whom I met first at the age of twenty-one. We became chums almost at once. He was the first to encourage me. I may say that he was my first protector. I never see him now, but as long as I live I shall never forget his kindness to me nor the debt that I owe him. He introduced me to his father; he worked with me in collaboration.

"My first real piece of work, however," he added, after a pause, "was a little comedy written in collaboration with Dumas *fils*, who was, and has remained, one of my best friends. Our play was called *Broken Straws*, and was acted at the Gymnase Theatre in Paris; but, although I much enjoyed light dramatic work, I did not find that it brought me anything in the way of substance or fortune.

"I was living then on a small pension allowed me by my father, and had dreams of wealth which led me into one or two speculations at the Bourse. These did not realize my dreams, I may add. But I derived some benefit from constant visits to the *coulisses* of the Bourse, for it was there that I got to know the romance of commerce, the fever of business, which I have often described and used in my novels.

"Whilst speculating at the Bourse, and collaborating with Hignard in operette and chanson, and with Alexandre Dumas in comedy, I contributed short stories to the magazines. My first work appeared in the *Musée des Familles* (*Family Museum*). There you can find `A Drama in the Air,' a story of mine about a madman in a balloon, which attracted some attention and is the first indication of the line of novel that I was destined to follow. I was then secretary to the Lyric Theatre, and afterwards secretary to M. Perrin. I adored the stage and all connected with it, and the work that I have enjoyed the most has been my writing for the stage.

"You know we have in France a proverb which declares that a man always ends by returning to his old love. Well, as I told you before, I always took a special delight in everything dramatic, and made my literary debut as a playwright, and of the many substantial satisfactions brought me by my labours, none gave more pleasure than my return to the stage. I have never lost my love for the stage and everything connected with theatrical life. One of the keenest joys my story-writing has brought me has been the successful staging of some of my novels."

"And which of your stories were most successful in dramatic form?"

"*Michel Strogoff* (*Michael Strogoff*) was perhaps the most popular; it was played all over the world; then *Le Tour du monde en quatre-vingts jours* (*Around the World in Eighty Days* was very successful, and more lately *Mathias Sandorf* was acted in Paris; it may amuse you to know further that my *Le Docteur Ox* (*Doctor Ox*) formed the basis of an operetta at the Varietes. I was once able to superintend the mounting of my pieces myself; now, my only glimpse of the theatrical world is seen from the front, in our charming Amiens theatre, on the, I must admit, frequent occasions when some good provincial company honours our town with its presence."

The interviews quoted above were originally published in English, from translations of Verne's remarks provided by the interviewers. For full citations and a definitive study of the subject, see Daniel Compère and Jean-Michel Margot, eds., *Entretiens avec Jules Verne 1873-1905* (Genève: Editions Slatkine, 1998).

Introduction

Jules Verne—the Successful, Wealthy Playwright

by Jean-Michel Margot

Although he is best known as a writer of extraordinary adventures, Jules Verne—one of the most translated novelists in the world—was also a prolific playwright. Until he achieved fame when Pierre-Jules Hetzel published his first novel, *Cinq Semaines en ballon* (*Five Weeks in a Balloon*, 1863), the majority of his literary activity was devoted to the theater. Verne's stage productions can be divided into three categories: the plays he wrote during his youth (before he met Hetzel), his operas and operettas, and the "pièces à grand spectacle" (great spectacle plays) inspired by his novels. This dramatic output, while generally unknown, was extensive, comprising some 38 plays: five historical dramas, 18 comedies and vaudevilles, eight libretti for opera-comiques and operettas, and seven plays written from his novels.

During his lifetime (1828–1905), Verne had only one publisher for his novels. Hetzel (1814–1886) was the most important French publisher of the 19th century, and also published Alphonse Daudet, Alexandre Dumas, Charles Dickens, George Sand, Victor Hugo, and Théophile Gautier. His illustrators were, among many others, Léon Benett, Emile Bayard, Bertall, Gustave Doré, Eugène Froment, Tony Johannot, and Ernest Meissonier. In 1873, he handed management of the publishing company to his son, Louis-Jules Hetzel, who inherited the firm upon the death of Pierre-Jules in 1886.

Verne's editor, Pierre-Jules Hetzel.

Between 1862 and 1875, Hetzel and Verne signed six contracts, which must be delineated in order to fully understand Verne's later writing for the stage.[1] The first contract, dated October 23, 1862—Verne lived in Paris, Passage Saulnier 18—dealt only with his first novel, *Five Weeks in a Balloon*, referred to in the contract as *Journey in the Air*. Two thousand copies were planned and Verne would receive 500 francs, which was about 8% of the sales price. If more copies were printed, Verne would get 0.25 franc per copy, as well as 5% of the sales price of every illustrated edition. This first contract doesn't mention any possible future novels or titles.

The second contract, dated January 1, 1864, was signed only after Verne delivered the first part of *Voyages et Aventures du capitaine Hatteras* (*Journeys and Adventures of Captain Hatteras*, 1866). Hetzel, who planned to begin publishing a fortnightly magazine for the French family, the *Magasin d'éducation et de recreation*, allowed Verne all of 1863 to work on *Hatteras* so that it would be ready for serialization the following year. Verne—who now lived at Rue de la Fontaine 39 in Auteuil, a suburb of Paris—received 3000 francs from a planned printing of 10,000 copies. Although this was less per copy than what he had made from *Five Weeks in a Balloon*, Verne received 0.30 francs for all future copies of *Hatteras* and 6% of the sales price of every illustrated edition, which was more than what was earned on his first novel. The contract also mentions two works to be written later, *Les Enfants du capitaine Grant* (*The Children of Captain Grant*, 1868), in three volumes, and *Histoire des grands voyages et des grands voyageurs* (*History of the Great Travels and Great Travelers*, 1880), in six volumes, with the stipulation that two volumes be delivered every year. Thus began the collaboration that made the Hetzel-Verne tandem unique in the history of French literature.

In fact, Verne didn't write *The Children of Captain Grant* or the *History of the Great Travels and Travelers* in 1864 and 1865. He finished *Journeys and Adventures of Captain Hatteras* and wrote *Voyage au centre de la Terre* (*Journey to the Center of the Earth*), published November 25, 1864, and *De la Terre à la Lune* (*From the Earth to the Moon*), published October 25, 1865. There was never a contract for these two titles and the third contract took care of the

---

1. Martin, Charles-Noël. *Jules Verne, sa vie et son oeuvre*. Lausanne: Rencontre, 1971.

lapse, with Verne receiving 300 francs every month for the five first volumes published. [2]

The third contract, dated December 11, 1865, made Verne—who still lived in Auteuil—a permanent, full-time employee of Hetzel. This six-year contract superseded all previous agreements. At that time, Hetzel didn't publish any illustrated editions, so the related clauses of the first two contracts were never applied. Verne was asked for three volumes per year, and Hetzel reserved the rights for himself for ten years after the publication of a novel. Then came what may be regarded as the abusive clause: "It is understood between Mr. Hetzel and Mr. Verne that the absolute and indefinite ownership of the works that are the object of this contract is transferred by Mr. Verne to Mr. Hetzel for the exploitation of those works in illustrated editions."

According to Hetzel's accounting for 1870, he earned 64,429.54 francs—eight times as much as Verne, who only received 7,666.70 francs. By choosing to receive monthly payments from Hetzel instead of a percentage of book sales, Verne lost huge amounts of money. Novels didn't make Verne rich.

The fourth contract, dated May 8, 1868, bound Verne to Hetzel for ten more years. By then, Verne was living in Le Crotoy, at the mouth of the river Somme, but he still kept an address in Paris. He was required to deliver three volumes a year and received 833.33 francs per month from Hetzel, who, once again, retained the rights to non-illustrated books for ten years after publication and assumed perpetual ownership of the illustrated editions. Thus, Verne received nothing from the shiny illustrated volumes, that are today among the most wanted collectibles.

Before meeting Hetzel in 1862, Verne published short stories in the magazine, *Musée des familles* (*Family Museum*). The fourth contract mentioned them and gave Verne the right to one such publication per year; some would be reprinted at the end of longer novels or as separate volumes. The fourth contract also stipulated that the *Géographie illustrée de la France et de ses colonies* (*Geography of France and its Colonies*, 1868), which Hetzel asked Verne to complete, was totally owned by Hetzel, the rights included in the monthly payments to Verne.

---

2. These five volumes are: *Five Weeks in a Balloon, Journey to the Center of the Earth, From the Earth to the Moon, Les Anglais au pôle Nord* (*The Englishmen at the North Pole*), and *Le Désert de glace* (*The Ice Desert*). The last two volumes form the two-volume novel *Journeys and Adventures of Captain Hatteras*. In the contracts and in their letters, Verne and Hetzel numbered the novelist's production in "volumes."

The three plays that made Verne wealthy—*Around the World in Eighty Days*, *Michael Strogoff*, and *The Children of Captain Grant*.

The fifth contract is lost, but it was summarized in the sixth contract. We therefore know that the fifth contract was signed September 25, 1871, and mainly modified two elements of the preceding contract: the monthly payments to Verne became 1,000.00 francs, and he had to deliver only two volumes per year instead of three.

The sixth and last contract with Hetzel was signed May 17, 1875. Verne had married Honorine Deviane, a widow with two daughters, in 1857, and with her had a son, Michel, in 1861. At the end of the decade, the family moved to Amiens, north of Paris, where Jules Verne spent the rest of his life. In twelve articles, the final contract confirmed the previous contracts, with two volumes to be delivered per year. It stipulated that the rights were to be equally divided between the publisher and the writer for all further serialization of the novels and for the translations. Also added were some considerations about the *Geography of France and its Colonies*, the *History of the Great Travels and Great Travelers*, and two new novels, *Michel Strogoff* (*Michael Strogoff*, 1876) and *Hector Servadac* (1877).

An awareness of Verne's secondary place as a novelist was reflected in the contemporary newspaper and magazine articles suggesting he was at least as well known as a playwright than novelist.[3] The day after Verne's death, in its March 25, 1905 issue, *The New York Times* echoed Verne's status as Hetzel's employee.

> An interesting story is passed around in French literary circles with regard to the contract by which Verne issued two books a year. It is said that this contract was made forty years ago, and called for two stories a year for a remuneration of 20,000 francs per annum or about $1,000. It is said that, despite the enormous circulation of his works, which have been translated even in Persian and Japanese, Jules Verne never received a penny more than his stipulated salary. His publisher, however, gave the author valuable presents from time to time.

What was the real relationship between the two men? Until recently, scholars and journalists could only speculate. Today there are available the volumes of correspondence between Verne and Hetzel,

---

3. Margot, Jean-Michel. *Jules Verne en son temps*. Amiens: Encrage, 2004.

Correspondance inédite de Jules Verne et de Pierre-Jules Hetzel, which allows a better understanding of the relationship between the publisher and his author—while also raising fresh questions.

In 1914, Hetzel's business was sold to Hachette, one of the leading French publishing firms, founded in 1824 and still in business today. Over half the value of Hetzel's shop was thanks to Verne. Hachette owned the rights to Verne's works until they fell into the public domain in the early 1960s.[4]

The sixth contract has two elements that were missing previously. Article 11 stipulates that all Verne plays have to be published by Hetzel. In return, Verne gave up his rights to the illustrated and non-illustrated editions of the first novels from *Five Weeks in a Balloon* to *L'Île mystérieuse* (*The Mysterious Island,* 1875) until January 1, 1882. Why does Verne postpone for seven years the additional money that would come from the previous non-illustrated editions?

A change in Verne's status occurred between the two last contracts. Verne had been an employee of Hetzel, just making a living; in the other, Verne became known (and well known) as a playwright. On November 7, 1874, not long before the last contract was signed, *Le Tour du monde en quatre-vingts jours* (*Around the World in Eighty Days*) premiered at the Théâtre de la Porte Saint-Martin in Paris. This successful production, staged a year after the publication of the novel of the same title, had a first run of 415 performances and began to make Jules Verne rich.

Verne of course continued to write novels for Hetzel, but he could now afford a yacht, something he had dreamed about since he was a teenager.[5] In March 1873, he bought a house in Amiens, and in 1877, he purchased the *Saint-Michel III,* a combined sailing and steam-ship with a crew of ten.

Why and how could Verne produce such successful plays? In the 1870s and 1880s, theatre and opera were the only entertainment. The

---

4. Dumas, Olivier. "Hetzel et Verne: 25 ans de collaboration." *Art & Métiers du Livre* (Paris), no 139 (May 1986), 49-55.

5. Verne, Jules. "Souvenirs d'enfance et de jeunesse". *Bulletin de la Société Jules Verne,* no. 89 (1989), 3–8. This text was sent to the U.S. by Verne in French and translated (almost adapted) into English to be published in Boston in *The Youth's Companion* on April 9, 1891, page 211. Two French manuscripts of this text exist—in Nantes and in Geneva—which were discovered later and published in French in 1974 and 1989.

The underground men of *Journey Through the Impossible*; illustration by Roger Leyonmark from the first American edition, reprinted by permission.

Third Republic, hoping to forget the Franco-Prussian War and Paris Commune, turned to plays and operas as the best escape. The dazzling and merciless school of "opéra-bouffe" from the Second Empire was replaced by pleasant and bourgeoisie productions of republican "opéra-comique," fairy plays and "pieces à grand spectacle" were flourishing.[6] *Around the World in Eighty Days* was typical of the latter; it is a geographic play that put on stage new landscapes, exotic people, live elephants and serpents, natural cataclysms, and strange vehicles that an audience could enjoy without leaving their seats. Nothing was neglected; grand spectacles, employing original ballets and music, sumptuous sets, and clever machinery, were precursors to the motion picture effects spectacular of the next century.

Verne wrote the stage version of *Around the World in Eighty Days* with Adolphe Philippe, alias Adolphe d'Ennery (also written Dennery) (1811-1899).   At the end of the 19th century in Paris, d'Ennery's collaboration was a guarantee of success, and he had as many as five presentations on the Paris stage at one time. As sole or part author of more than 280 plays, he is best known for *Les Deux Orphelines* (*The Two Orphans*, 1875). His plays were mainly written in collaboration with others, including Alexandre Dumas *père* and Verne for the text, and Jules Massenet for the music.

D'Ennery also helped Verne bring to the stage *The Children of Captain Grant, Michael Strogoff,* and *Voyage à travers l'impossible* (*Journey Through the Impossible*). *The Children of Captain Grant* and *Michael Strogoff* were inspired by the novels of the same title and, like their predecessor, all three became hits on the American stage. Later, alone and with other collaborators, Verne adapted his novels *Kéraban-le-têtu* (*Keraban the Inflexible*, 1883) and *Mathias Sandorf* (1887) for the theatre.

Journey Through the Impossible was on stage in Paris at the "Théâtre de la Porte Saint-Martin," where *Around the World in Eighty Days* played eight years earlier, on November 25, 1882. The play was presented 97 times (43 in 1882 and 54 in 1883). For more than a century the text of the play was considered lost. No Verne manuscript was left and only reviews survived until a copy was discovered in the

---

6.   Pourvoyeur, Robert. "Jules Verne et le théâtre". In Verne, Jules. *Clovis Dardentor.* Paris: Union générale d'éditions (coll. *10/18*, no 1308), série *Jules Verne inattendu,* 1979, pp. 5–30.

Archives of the Censorship Office of the Third Republic in 1978. (The Censorship Office was a relic of the Second Empire and every play was copied by anonymous clerks before it could be performed.)

Journey Through the Impossible is unique among all Verne's work for containing the most science fiction elements, and it is an original, not an adaptation of a previously published novel. The title, *Journey Through the Impossible*, suggests a fundamental departure from all of Verne's other work; his novels were published under the broader title of "Voyages Extraordinaires" ("Extraordinary Journeys"). This time, the journey is no longer extraordinary—it is impossible.

Often in Verne's novels, the heroes never reach their goal; in *Journey to the Center of the Earth*, they travel under the Earth's surface, never reaching the center. Michel Ardan, Impey Barbicane, and Nicholl travel *From the Earth to the Moon* without landing on our satellite. However, the travelers of *Journey Through the Impossible* reach their goals. Between a prolog and an epilog, the hero goes to the center of the Earth in the first act, to the bottom of the seas in the second act, and travels to the Planet Altor in the third. In 1904, when interviewed by the British journalist Gordon Jones and asked about the science in his novels, Verne said, "But these results are merely the natural outcome of the scientific trend of modern thought, and as such have doubtless been predicted by scores of others besides myself. Their coming was inevitable, whether anticipated or not, and the most that I can claim is to have looked perhaps a little farther into the future than the majority of my critics."[7] And yet *Journey Through the Impossible*, performed over two decades earlier, contradicts this statement.

Written with the same structure as *Les Contes d'Hoffman* (*The Tales of Hoffmann*, 1881), where Hoffmann has to choose between love and art, *Journey Through the Impossible* is the struggle between love and knowledge. The hero of the *Impossible* is George Hatteras, the son of Captain Hatteras who discovered the North Pole in *Journeys and Adventures of Captain Hatteras* in 1866. George has to choose between love and knowledge, good and evil, happiness and science. The tempter is Doctor Ox, resurrected by Verne from the short story *Doctor Ox*. The Guardian Angel is Volsius, who becomes Otto Lidenbrock (the

---

7.   "Jules Verne at Home". *Temple Bar* (London), No. 129 (June 1904), 664-71.

main character of the *Journey to the Center of the Earth*) in the first act; Nemo (the captain of *Vingt mille lieues sous les mers* [*Twenty Thousand Leagues under the Seas*, 1870]) in the second act, and Michel Ardan (astronaut in *From the Earth to the Moon*) in the third act. Not inventing new characters, Verne took existing heroes from the "Extraordinary Journeys" and let them travel "through the impossible." George Hatteras is with his fiancée, Eva, who shares his adventures. This is another distinction from Verne's works, where usually the women stay home and dispatch the hero on his extraordinary journey. Eva helps Volsius save George from the evil knowledge of science that is offered to him by Doctor Ox.

Alexandre Dumas, *père*, in the 1860s.

Verne wrote *Journey Through the Impossible* at the turning point of his life and his literary career. In the first half of his life, he wrote novels and plays where science was viewed positively, and engineers and scientists were mainly working for the future of mankind. The typical character of this first period is Cyrus Smith, the engineer of *The Mysterious Island*. In the second half of his life, Verne wrote novels (and almost no additional plays) where science was questionable, and used by evil characters to create misfortune among people, such as Robur in *Maître du monde* (*Master of the World*, 1904) and the titular figure in *Le Secret de Wilhelm Storitz* (*The Secret of Wilhelm Storitz*, 1910).

Hence, in many ways, *Journey Through the Impossible* was one of the most intriguing, surprising, and important works of Jules Verne. That's why it was the first book published by the North American Jules Verne Society, through Prometheus, in 2003. Now, in the Palik series, the Society offers a volume of Verne's more youthful plays, in several genres, that in many ways anticipate the novels of his maturity.

Verne had begun his literary career as a playwright, not as novelist. When he met Hetzel in 1862, at age 34, Verne had written more than two dozen theatrical pieces. Some of them were on stage and published, and some still await publication today. These first theatrical pieces were never very successful.

Verne's biographers mention several plays, both tragedies and vaudeville-like comedies, written before he was twenty. At age seventeen, Verne supposedly submitted a tragedy in verse to a puppet theater in Nantes, his birthplace. The piece was rejected, which is all that we know; the text is lost and even the title is unknown. In 1848, at the age of twenty, Verne was sent to Paris by his father to attend law school (he graduated in 1850 with a *licence en droit*). The young Verne's first priority, however, was to become known in theatrical circles.

Through one of his uncles, Verne met Alexandre Dumas *père* (1802-1870). One of the most famous French writers of the nineteenth century, he is best known today for historical adventure novels, including the sagas of the Three Musketeers, and the Count of Monte Cristo. He "adopted" Verne, who so impressed him that, forty years later, Alexandre Dumas *fils* wrote to say that Verne was, more than himself, the true son of the elder Dumas. Alexandre Dumas the younger, 1824-1895, also a playwright and novelist, was the illegitimate son of his father, and

Alexandre Dumas, *fils*.

became famous for comedies of manners, but is best remembered for *La Dame aux camélias*, known in English as *Camille*.

Dumas *père* opened his Théâtre Historique with *La Jeunesse des Mousquetaires* (*The Youth of the Musketeers*) on February 17, 1849, with Verne as a guest in Dumas's own box. In the dedication to Verne's first staged play, *Les Pailles rompues* (*The Broken Straws*, 1850), he expressed his gratitude to Dumas *fils*, who with his father, assisted in writing and staging the play in his theater. This short play is a witty and affected conversation between a coquettish woman and her jealous husband. It was inspired by Pierre Carlet de Chamblain de Marivaux (1688-1763), playwright and novelist, popular for his numerous comedies analyzing the sentiments and complications of love in a graceful, albeit often precious, style.

After Marivaux, Verne explored dramatic possibilities with Alfred de Musset (1810-1857) as a model. A Romantic playwright, Musset is best remembered for his poetry, but much influenced by Shakespeare and Schiller, he wrote the first modern dramas in the French language. Verne wrote *Leonardo da Vinci* in 1851, and he labored at it on and off until reading it as *Monna Lisa* to the Académie d'Amiens in 1874 (with its first publication a century later). In Verne's *Monna Lisa*, a bittersweet explanation of the sibylline smile of La Giaconda, Leonardo is so immersed in his art that he forgets the beautiful Lisa, who would so willingly respond to his slightest attention. The description of Leonardo, unskillful with the woman he still loves, is a metaphor for Verne, the shy introvert.

Verne acknowledged that Michel Carré (1819-1872) helped him write the *Vinci* play. A successful French writer of libretti, Carré worked with Gounod, Offenbach, Meyerbeer, and Bizet, and with the poet and librettist Jules Barbier (1825-1901) to produce many well-known French operas between 1850 and 1870. In 1851, Barbier and Carré brought to the Odéon a fantastic drama, *Les Contes fantastiques d'Hoffman* (*The Fantastic Tales of Hoffmann*), and in 1881 Jacques Offenbach produced his own version, the last and one of the most remarkable French "opéras comiques." The comic opera is an exclusively French style of opera that evolved from earlier popular shows performed by troupes entertaining spectators at fairs. An "opéra comique" consists of spoken dialogue alternating with musical numbers, including arias and orchestral music. The Opéra-Comique theater in Paris was founded in 1715, with a repertoire of such works as Mozart's *Cosi Fan Tutte*, Donizetti's *La Fille du Régiment*, Berlioz's *Les Troyens*, Bizet's *Carmen*, Offenbach's *Les Contes d'Hoffmann*, Verdi's *Falstaff*, and Debussy's *Pelléas et Melisande*.

In the 1850s, it was common to stage so-called "comedy proverbs," short pieces that illustrated various proverbs. One such piece written by Verne remained unstaged, but it was published in 1852 in *Musée des familles* under the title of *Les Châteaux en Californie, ou, Pierre qui roule n'amasse pas mousse* (*The Castles in California, or, A Rolling Stone Gathers No Moss*). In this piece, Verne played with words and told jokes that, while perhaps innocent, nevertheless were often full of racy humor.

Taking advantage of similar sounding words such as *coeur* (heart) and *queue* (tail), Verne inserted many double meanings into his text. The most astonishing fact is that such a play was printed in the serious *Musée des familles*, whose target readership necessarily also included children.

In *Les Heureux du jour* (*Happy for One Day*, finished in 1856), Verne criticized Parisian society, ridiculing its vanity and greed. His style was already more mature and his writing more solid than in previous works.

Many scholars and biographers rightly insist on Verne's strong interest in music. So it is no wonder that the future novelist should insert music into his plays, producing pieces such as operas, operettas, and "opéras comiques." In so doing he was completely of his time, since operas were considered to be the highest form of both music and theater. In his novels as well, Verne often makes references to musical pieces, mainly to operas. Characters and narrators in his novels often quote the operas and operettas of his time, some of which are still well known today, while others have been completely forgotten. There are eighteen instances in *Claudius Bombarnac* (1892); even in *L'Île à hélice* (*Propeller Island*, 1895), several pages are dedicated to Mozart and Gounod's study of *Don Juan*.

Aristide Hignard (1822-1898), like Verne, was born in Nantes, and the two had apartments on the same floor in Paris. In the meantime, Dumas lost his Théâtre Historique, which was remodeled and named the Théâtre Lyrique in 1852. The new director, Edmond Sébastien Seveste, was looking for a secretary. Verne was hired on the recommendation of Dumas and Adrien Talexy (1821-1880), a French composer of popular music, mainly polkas and mazurkas. Shortly thereafter, Seveste died, and his brother, Jules-Henri, took over the direction of the Théâtre Lyrique, but died two years later, leaving Verne unemployed. So, with his first job, Verne was directly confronted with the life of the theater, with the various personalities of its musicians and artists, with financial problems, and with bills to pay. It is likely that he did a good job: some fifty pieces were staged over three years.

Verne's own first musical piece performed on stage is an "opéra comique" in one act, *Le Colin-Maillard* (*The Blind Man's Bluff*, 1853). Inspired by Beaumarchais's *Le Mariage de Figaro* (*The Marriage of Figaro*), and with the collaboration of Michel Carré, the plot involves four couples playing the title game in the woods on a Sunday afternoon.

The Théâtre Lyrique in Verne's time.

In 1860 Verne was back on stage at the Théâtre Lyrique with another show written with Carré and Hignard, *L'Auberge des Ardennes* (*The Inn of the Ardennes*). This "opéra comique" uses the familiar situation of an inn with no rooms available. A young newlywed wants a room for himself and his bride and the only solution is to frighten another tourist into fleeing and making his room available. Of course, the other tourist is an attorney who has papers that will make the newlywed wealthy. If Lecoq, who specialized in comedies about thwarted wedding nights, had written the music instead of Hignard, perhaps *The Inn of the Ardennes* would still be on stage today.

Un Neveu d'Amérique, ou, les deux Frontignac (*An American Nephew, or, the Two Frontignacs*) was written in 1861. Staged in 1873 at the Théâtre Cluny, it was published by Hetzel in 1873. Based upon the original and hilarious idea of taking out a life annuity and death insurance on the same character, it is without a doubt Verne's best play. The brilliantly funny yet natural dialogue is delivered at breakneck speed even as it maintains the depth of the characters.

By this point, Verne had explored several literary routes (plays, operas, operettas, and *opéras comiques*) and fully mastered the playwright's skills. *An American Nephew*, an excellent satiric work, suggests what kind of playwright Verne could have become with a little more maturity and experience. But Verne's fateful meeting with Hetzel was just around the corner and Verne's literary career was destined to explore "Known and Unknown Worlds," to recall the subtitle of the "Extraordinary Journeys." At age 34, Verne became a novelist, but he would return to playwriting once he became a best-selling author. His was a circular path, that led to success in both stage and in print.

The Theatrical Works
of Jules Verne

Titles, in both French and English, are organized chronologically. Annotations include the following information: a) type of work (e.g., comedy, tragedy, opera); b) possible Verne collaborators; c) date and place of the premiere performance; d) number of first-run performances; e) miscellaneous comments; and f) publication information where relevant (*BSJV = Bulletin de la Société Jules Verne*).

1845

Untitled verse tragedy; for the Puppet Théâtre Riquiqui in Nantes; the text, mentioned in biographies, is lost.

Untitled vaudeville piece; only Act 2 remains.

1847

Alexandre VI; five-act verse tragedy; dated mid-1847; alternate title: *Cesar Borgia*.

1848

La Conspiration des poudres (*The Powder Conspiracy*); five-act verse tragedy.

Une Promenade en mer (*An Excursion at Sea*); one-act vaudeville piece.

Le Quart d'heure de Rabelais (*The Fifteen Minutes of Rabelais*); one-act verse comedy.

Don Galaor; one-act comedy.

1849

Les Pailles rompues (*The Broken Straws*); one-act verse comedy; possible collaboration with Alexandre Dumas, both *père* and *fils*; premiered at the Théâtre Historique on June 12, 1850; 12 or 15 performances through June 25, 1850; revival in Nantes on November 7, 1850; revival at the Théâtre du Gymnase from 1853 to 1857 (45 performances); revival at the Théâtre du Gymnase in 1871 and 1872 (40 performances); published by Beck (1850), and in *Revue Jules Verne* 11 (2001): 33-94.

Un Drame sous Louis XV (*A Drama under Louis XV*); five-act verse tragedy; alternate title: *A Drama under the Regency*.

Abd'allah; two-act vaudeville piece.

Le Coq de bruyère (*The Wood Grouse*).

On a souvent besoin d'un plus petit que soi (*Little Friends May Prove Great Friends*).

1850

La Guimard (*The Guimard*); two-act comedy.

Quiridine et Quiridnerit (*When Love Dines*); three-act "Italian Comedy" in verse.

La Mille et deuxième nuit (*The Thousand and Second Night*); one-act libretto; music by Aristide Hignard.

1851

Les Savants (*The Scholars*); three-act "Observation Comedy"; manuscript is lost.

Les Fiancés bretons (*The Fiancés of Britanny*); manuscript is lost.

De Charybde en Scylla (From Charybdis to Scylla); comic one-act "Character Study" in verse.

Monna Lisa (1851-1855); one-act verse comedy; reading at the Academy of Amiens on May 22, 1874; alternate titles: *The Jocund, Leonardo da Vinci*; published in *Cahiers de l'Herne* (Paris 1974); published by L'Herne (1995).

Les Châteaux en Californie, ou, Pierre qui roule n'amasse pas mousse (*Castles in California, or A Rolling Stone Gathers No Moss*); one-act proverb comedy; collaboration with Pitre-Chevalier; staged in Torino, Italy, on April 28, 1969; published in *Musée des familles* (June 1852).

1852

La Tour de Montlhéry (*Tower of Monthléry*); five-act drama; collaboration with Charles Wallut.

Le Colin-Maillard (*The Blind Man's Bluff*); one-act "opéra comique"; collaboration with Michel Carré; music by Aristide Hignard; premiered at the Théâtre lyrique on April 28, 1853; 45 performances; libretto published by Lévy (1853); score published by Alfred Ikelmer (1853); published in *BSJV* 120 (1996).

1853

Les Compagnons de la Marjolaine (*The Knights of the Daffodil*, or *The Companions of Marjoram*); one-act "opéra comique"; collaboration with Michel Carré; music by Aristide Hignard; premiered at the Théâtre lyrique on June 6, 1855; 24 performances; libretto published by Lévy (1855); published in *BSJV* 143 (2002)>.

Les Heureux du jour (*Happy for One Day*, 1855-1856); five-act comic "Study of Manners" in verse.

1854

Guerre aux tyrans (*War on Tyrants*); one-act verse comedy.

1855

Au bord de l'Adour (*Beside the Adour*); one-act verse comedy.[1]

1857

Monsieur de Chimpanzé (*Mr. Chimpanzee*); one-act operetta; possible collaboration with Michel Carré; music by Aristide Hignard; premiered at the Bouffes-Parisiens on February 17, 1858; ran until March 3, 1858; published in *BSJV* 57 (1981).

1858

Le Page de Madame Marlbrough (*Madame Marlbrough's Page*); one-act operetta; written under the pseudnoym E. Vierne; music by Frédéric Barbier; premiered at the Théâtre des Folies-Nouvelles on October 28, 1858; alternate incorrect title: *Une Robe de Madame Malbrough* (*A Dress of Madame Malbrough*).

1859

L'Auberge des Ardennes (*The Inn of the Ardennes*); one-act "opéra comique"; collaboration with Michel Carré; music by Aristide Hignard; premiered at the Théâtre lyrique on September 1, 1860 (20 performances); published by Lévy (1860).

---

1. The Adour is a river marking the border between France and Spain, flowing into the Biscay Gulf.

1860

Onze jours de siège (*Eleven Days of Siege*, 1854-1860); three-act comedy; collaboration with Charles Wallut; premiered at the Théâtre du vaudeville on June 1, 1861; published by Lévy (1861).

Un Fils adoptif (*The Adoptive Son*); comedy; collaboration with Charles Wallut; broadcast on French radio on April 5, 1950; published in *BSJV* 140 (2001).

1861

Un Neveu d'Amérique ou les deux Frontignac (*An American Nephew, or, The Two Frontignacs*); three-act comedy; perhaps reworked by Edouard Cadol and Eugène Labiche; premiered at the Théâtre Cluny on April 17, 1873; ran for two months; published by Hetzel (1873); published with *Clovis Dardentor* (10/18, 1979).

1867

Les Sabines (*The Sabines*, 1857, 1867); "opéra-bouffe," or two- or three-act operetta (only the first act still exists); collaboration with Charles Wallut.

1871

Le Pôle Nord (*The North Pole*).

1873

Le Tour du monde en 80 jours (*Around the World in 80 Days*, 1873-1874); five-act "pièce à grand spectacle" with prologue (15 tableaux); collaboration with Adolphe d'Ennery; music by J.-J. Debillemont; premiered at the Théâtre de la Porte Saint-Martin on November 7, 1874 (415 performances); published by Hetzel (1879).

1875

Les Enfants du capitaine Grant (*The Children of Captain Grant*); five-act "pièce à grand spectacle" with prologue (13 tableaux); collaboration with Adolphe d'Ennery; music by J.-J. Debillemont; premiered at the Théâtre de la Porte Saint-Martin on December 26, 1878 (113 performances); published by Hetzel (1881).

1877

Le Docteur Ox (*Doctor Ox*); three-act "opéra-bouffe" (6 tableaux); libretto by Philippe Gille and Arnold Mortier (with Verne's approval); music by Jacques Offenbach; premiered at the Théâtre des Variétés (42 performances).

1878

Michael Strogoff; five-act "pièce à grand spectacle" with prologue (16 tableaux); collaboration with Adolphe d'Ennery; premiered at the Théâtre du Châtelet on November 17, 1880 (386 performances); published by Hetzel (1881).

1882

Voyage à travers l'impossible (*Journey Through the Impossible*); three-act fantasy "pièce à grand spectacle" (20 tableaux); collaboration with Adolphe d'Ennery; music by Oscar de Lagoanère; premiered at the Théâtre de la Porte Saint-Martin on November 25, 1882 (43 performances in 1882; 54 performances in 1883); published in Paris by Pauvert (1981).

1883

Kéraban-le-Têtu (*Keraban the Inflexible*); five-act play (20 tableaux); premiered at the Théâtre de la Gaîté lyrique on September 3, 1883 (49 performances); published in *BSJV* 85-86 (1988).

Les Erreurs d'Alcide (*Errors of Alcide*); missing three-act comedy for the Théâtre Cluny; written in collaboration with Emile Abraham and Gustave Maurens; details first published in *Verniana*, 2 (2009-2010).

1888

Les Tribulations d'un Chinois en Chine (*The Tribulations of a Chinese in China*); the manuscript is lost; collaboration declined by Adolphe d'Ennery, subsequently dramatized by Claude Farrère and Charles Méré without Verne's participation.

The theater, music, and spectacle were central to the life and stories of Jules Verne.

615. AMIENS (Somme) - Le Cirque (une des curiosités de la Picardie).
R.P.   The Circus (one of the curiossitées of Picardy).

PROST, éd', Amie

As a town councilman in Amiens, Verne persuaded the city to build a circus seating 4000 for the benefit of traveling shows that came to town.

The strange source of musical notes in a church organ is featured in
"M. Ré-Dièze et Mlle. Mi-Bémol" ("Mr. D Sharp and Miss E Flat," 1893).

The worlds of the gothic and scientific devices for the audio-visual recording of performances collide in *The Castle in the Carpathians* (1892).

A measure of the changes wrought by *Doctor Ox* (1872) becomes a fast-paced opera.

Musicians are abducted to perform on *L'Île à hélice*
(*Propeller Island*, 1895).

Stranded in Japan, Passepartout joins the Long Noses in *Le Tour du monde en quatre-vingts jours* (*Around the World in Eighty Days*, 1873).

A traveling circus provides refuge in *Mathias Sandorf* (1885).

This 1890 novel was an affectionate tribute to a troupe of circus performers.

Invading Tartars offer spectacle in *Michael Strogoff* (1876).

The Orientalist view of the Far East is at the center of *Les Tribulations d'un Chinois en Chine* (*The Tribulations of a Chinese in China*, 1879).

THE KNIGHTS OF THE DAFFODIL
(The Companions of Marjoram)

Aristide Hignard, Courtesy Volker Dehs Collection.

*L*es *Compagnons de la Marjolaine* is an "opéra-comique" in one act. The title has been translated here as *The Knights of the Daffodil* to best convey, in English, the spirit of the original, although a more literal rendering would be *The Companions of Marjoram*. Verne wrote it 1853 with Michel Carré; Aristide Hignard provided the music. It opened June 6, 1855, at the Théâtre-Lyrique (Lyric Theater), and ran for 24 performances. The Théâtre-Lyrique had a capacity of 1700 seats, and opened in 1847 under the name Théâtre Historique (History Theater), sponsored by Alexandre Dumas to promote theatrical adaptations of his novels; it closed in 1863. *Les Compagnons de la Marjolaine* was published that year as a 29 page booklet in Paris by Michel Lévy frères.

In the play, Boniface, owner of the inn at St. Paterno, dominated by his wife, does not want his daughter Marceline to marry the ferryman Simplice: he is cowardly, foolish, and worst of all—he is poor. Simplice must discover his courage when Marceline becomes the target of the "Knights of the Daffodil," young men who go from village to village, abducting women, drinking the best wine, and thrashing any reluctant hosts.

In 1853, the first comic opera by Verne, Carré, and Hignard, *Le Colin-maillard* (*The Blind Man's Bluff*), was presented at the Théâtre-Lyrique, where Verne was secretary. The opening of *The Knights of the Daffodil* had already been delayed the following year, and with the death of its director, the theater, lacking a government subsidy, faced an uncertain future. The play was regarded as amusing and successful by critics, with a harmonic, lively gait, and marked a sharp improvement over *The Blind*

Man's Bluff. Most impressive is the quality of the lyrics; the verse is freer, more inspired, suggesting the melodies. The subject is less convoluted, and the psychology of the characters has a greater realism. At the same time, the outlaws predictably undergo a radical about-face.

French composer Jean-Louis Aristide Hignard was the son of a ship owner, born on May 20, 1822, who died on March 20, 1898. He would likely be completely forgotten, were he not befriended by Verne. Both from Nantes, they found themselves next door in Paris and lived a bohemian life, punctuated by meals of "Onze-sans-femmes" ("Eleven-without-women"). Verne and Hignard undertook two journeys, one in England and Scotland in 1859 and another in Scandinavia in 1861; the former was lightly fictionalized in *Voyage à reculons en Angleterre et en Ecosse* (*Journey to England and Scotland*, 1859), where Hignard is called Jonathan Savournon. He collaborated with Jules Verne on the opéra-comiques, and signed some of his songs.

In Paris, Hignard was a pupil of Jacques Fromental Halevy at the Conservatory, and became a teacher and gave lessons to Emmanuel Chabrier. In 1850, he won the second grand prix de Rome music, and the following year, presented a comic opera in one act, *Le Visionnaire* (*The Visionary*). In 1868, he wrote *Hamlet,* an opera from Shakespeare, and was awarded the prize of the Académie des beaux-arts (Academy of Fine Arts) in 1871. Success was short-lived, however, when his *Hamlet* was replaced in popular memory by another by Ambroise Thomas (1811-1896), an "opéra comique" also based on the Shakespeare play. Hignard's opera was not presented again until 1888, at the Théâtre Graslin in Nantes. Modest, shy, reluctant to advertise, he died, cared for by his wife, in 1898 in Vernon, where he had retired. More recently, some of his melodies have been released on a CD celebrating his collaboration with Verne.

The other plays by Verne and Hignard include *La Mille et deuxième nuit* (*The Thousand and Second Night*, 1850), never staged; *Mr. Chimpanzee*; and *L'Auberge des Ardennes* (*The Inn of the Ardennes*, 1860), an opéra-comique by Verne and Carré. The prolific French librettist Michel Carré was born October 20, 1821, in Besançon, and died June 27, 1872, in Argenteuil. He went to Paris in 1840 intending to become a painter, but followed a different muse, composing verse and plays before turning to libretti. He became best known for his collaborations with Jules Barbier on numerous operas, usually adaptations of existing literary masterworks.

Michel Carré, Courtesy Volker Dehs Collection.

An illustration for the 1882 Italian edition of
The Knights of the Daffodil.

CHARACTERS

SIMPLICE, a ferryman of the St-Romans on the Isere ferry

GUERFROID, a wine grower

LANDRY, a shepherd

BONIFACE, an innkeeper

MARCELINE, his daughter

DAME MONIQUE, his wife

The action takes place in the village of Saint-Romans in Languedoc. The stage represents a low hall in the inn of Saint Paterne. At the back a double door, opening on the river Isere. To the right of this door a window; to the left, the opening of a wine room furnished with casks both empty and full. Side doors on the right and left. Tables and benches.

(MARCELINE is listening to the voice of Simplice in the distance.)

SIMPLICE: Pretty one, before the day is over
We will reach the beach.
Come, before the end of the day
We'll chat about love on the beach.

MARCELINE: *(running in)* Ah! Thank God! I hear him. Here he is!

(Marceline listens.)

SIMPLICE: There, we'll talk about intended love.
A nice pastime for the one who loves you!
There, we'll talk about love
From sundown to sun up.

MARCELINE: Ah! Thank God!
  He's here!

(She opens the door.)

SIMPLICE: *(entering)* I am here!

TOGETHER:

SIMPLICE:	MARCELINE:
My courage astonishes me!	His courage astonishes me!
Tonight, I'm no longer afraid.	Tonight he's no longer afraid.
It's love that gives me	It's love that gives him
Courage.	Courage.

SIMPLICE: If Mr. Boniface
  Separates us and runs me off,
  I'll laugh at his threats,
  I'll stare him in the face.

MARCELINE: In the face!

SIMPLICE: In the face!

MARCELINE: Like this!

SIMPLICE: Like this!

MARCELINE: Less boldly.

SIMPLICE: Like that.

MARCELINE: More politely.

SIMPLICE: With effrontery,
  Insolently,
  Proudly.

MARCELINE: *(aside)* What a change.

TOGETHER:

SIMPLICE:	MARCELINE:
My courage astonishes me!	His courage astonishes me!
Tonight, I'm no longer afraid.	Tonight he's no longer afraid.
It's love that gives me	It's love that gives him
Courage.	Courage.

MONIQUE: *(entering)* What have I seen?

SIMPLICE: *(terrified)* Heaven!

MARCELINE: *(retaining him)* Well!

MONIQUE: What are you doing in my home?

SIMPLICE: I—

MONIQUE: Speak!

MARCELINE: *(low to Simplice)* Well go on, speak!

SIMPLICE: I—I, so much the worse—my word! *(pointing to Marceline)* To my love I am coming to pay a visit.

MONIQUE: Eh! What!
By my holy patroness!
Miss is giving
A gallant rendez-vous.
In our home!
Let's go find her father;
He will know, I hope,
How to run this man
Out of here.

TOGETHER:

SIMPLICE:	**MARCELINE**:
Go find her father	Go find my father,
And, despite him, I hope,	He will not dare, I hope,
Not to leave here.	To send him away from here.

(Monique leaves.)

MARCELINE: If my father runs you off,
You laugh at his grimaces,
You brave his threats,
Confront him in his face.

SIMPLICE: In his face!

MARCELINE: In his face!

SIMPLICE: In his face.

MARCELINE: Like this—

SIMPLICE: Less boldly.

MARCELINE: Like that.

SIMPLICE: More politely.

MARCELINE: With effrontery,
  Insolently,
  Proudly.

SIMPLICE: *(aside)* Annoying moment!

TOGETHER:

SIMPLICE:	MARCELINE:
(aside) Despite myself I'm shivering,	*(aside)* Audacity abandons him,
I feel my heart beating,	I feel his heart beating,
Audacity abandons me,	There he is shivering,
I'm afraid.	He's afraid.

(Monique returns with Boniface who is armed with a stick.)

MONIQUE: There he is!

BONIFACE: Get out of here!

SIMPLICE: Dear Mr. Boniface!

BONIFACE: Get out of here!—I'm running you off!

MARCELINE: *(low to Simplice)* There you are, face to face!

SIMPLICE: What must I do?

MARCELINE: *(low)* Stay put!

BONIFACE: Begone!

MARCELINE: Speak.

BONIFACE: Shut up, you.

SIMPLICE: I—

BONIFACE: Huh?

MARCELINE: Will you say something!

SIMPLICE: I—I, so much the worse, my word! *(pointing to Marceline)* I am coming to ask for your little girl.

BONIFACE: Eh, what! Can one understand
  Such a demand
  Without suddenly
  Raising his hand!
  Since he's staying, I intend,
  With this stick, to pommel him
  On the subject, by the hour
  On his back.

TOGETHER:

SIMPLICE:	MARCELINE:	MONIQUE AND BONIFACE:
(aside) If I stay, he's going To drub me by the hour! *(reaching the back)* Let's turn our back On their proposal.	*(retaining him)* Stay still, stay! And don't go on the spot To turn your back.	It's necessary since he's staying With this stick, on the spot, To drub him on his back.

BONIFACE AND MONIQUE:	SIMPLICE:	MARCELINE:
Let's go! Show us your heels Or we will thrash you. We will beat you with a stick!	*(aside)* Let's go! Soon we will return And we shall see.	*(aside)* Let's go! Cursed be cowards. Cursed be cowards.

(Simplice escapes by the rear.)

BONIFACE: *(drying his face)* Ah! The wise guy!

MARCELINE: There, he's gone!

BONIFACE: To dare to introduce himself into my home to romance my daughter—

MONIQUE: It's your fault, too. I always told you. You don't know how to make either your daughter or your wife respected. And if I weren't here—If I didn't get involved sometimes, God knows what would happen.

BONIFACE: Monique, my dear Monique, let's not quarrel.

MONIQUE: Go, go, Mr. Boniface—you don't deserve a wife like me—

BONIFACE: It's true, that there are only compliments to be made to Monique on her wisdom and her good health.

MARCELINE: The fact is that nobody has a face as vermilion as hers!

MONIQUE: I boast of it! And here are two strong arms which will know how to protect me, if needed, from gallants. *(to Marceline)* As for Simplice, he has only to set his foot here again—and I will take it upon myself to throw him out the window, —On that, goodnight. *(she leaves)*

BONIFACE: She's right. That cursed boatman deserves a good beating!

MARCELINE: Why? For having dared to ask for the hand of your daughter?

BONIFACE: Him, my son-in-law! A coward—who's afraid of me!

MARCELINE: He's only a coward because he doesn't have a wife to protect him.

BONIFACE: A ninny.

MARCELINE: A ninny because he's in love.

BONIFACE: A poor devil of a boatman who has only his boat.

MARCELINE: His wife will bring him what he lacks.

BONIFACE: Shut up!

MARCELINE: I'm shutting up.

BONIFACE: Oh! Triple dummy that I am! *(striking his head)* Stupid donkey!

MARCELINE: What's the matter?

BONIFACE: How could I have forgotten. *(calling)* Hola! Tomassin! Andeol! *(enter two valets)* Quick! Tables! Mugs!

MARCELINE: What's the matter, my God?

BONIFACE: It's that—It's that—The Knights of the Daffodil have retained this room for tonight—and that they could come from one moment to the next.

MARCELINE: The Knights of the Daffodil!

BONIFACE: A troupe of young wise guys who go from village to village seducing the wives, carrying off the girls, drinking the best wines of the wine cellars, and roughing up recalcitrant inn keepers. They recognize each other by their Daffodils!

MARCELINE: Wow! *(aside)* My! My! My!

BONIFACE: They are coming tonight for the fest of Saint Severin,— and they have to gather here, at nightfall, to cross to the other side of the river. *(mysteriously)* The wine grower Guerfroid and Landry the shepherd have told me they will be the first to arrive, and they advised me to fill the mugs in advance. *(taking two mugs from the table)* That's what I'm going into the cellar for. *(heading towards the wine room)* As for you, do me the pleasure of going to your room.

MARCELINE: But, father—

BONIFACE: You will tell your stepmother to do it, also.

MARCELINE: Yes, father.

(Boniface exits.)

MARCELINE: *(alone, going to open the door)* See if Simplice has come back! If he was only half as brave as Dame Monique. *(sings)*
Oh, what a bore to love a timid lad.
Wouldn't it be a hundred times better
If he were intrepid?
To boldly raise his eyes!
If they marry us,
Does he want them to laugh
At his clumsiness?
Alas! Such a fiancé
The world's upside down.
If the spouse is wise
In his household,
He keeps power undivided.
It's a good custom,

And it's a great shame,
When, by chance, we usurp it.
Plague on husbands who wear the skirts!

   (ii)
Oh, what a bore to love such a timid lad!
Who's going to protect the house
If fear makes him an invalid
And deprives him of his reason!
If some tender lover
Comes to surprise me,
So much the worse for a husband too slow
Who allows a gallant to do whatever.
If the husband is wise
He keeps all the power undivided.
It's a good custom
Because it's a great shame,
When by chance, we usurp it.
Plague on all husbands who wear the skirts!

(Simplice jumps precipitously through the window.)

MARCELINE: God!

SIMPLICE: Hush! It's me!

MARCELINE: Ah! What a fright you gave me.

SIMPLICE: I just met two men down there who are heading this way, and I came to warn you.

MARCELINE: What's the good?

SIMPLICE: You don't know that I recognized them by their Daffodils!

MARCELINE: Ah, bah! They are the happy companions that my father was telling me about just now.

SIMPLICE: Frightful good for nothings!

MARCELINE: Charming lads!

SIMPLICE: Who respect nothing.

MARCELINE: Who are afraid of no one!

SIMPLICE: Who drink, who swear as if damned!

MARCELINE: Who know how to protect their loves!

SIMPLICE: You wouldn't want me to be like them!

MARCELINE: You wouldn't do so badly, if you already resembled them a bit.

SIMPLICE: Me!

MARCELINE: In your place, I would ask them to take a role in their band for a while!

SIMPLICE: What! You want?

MARCELINE: And if it's necessary for that to prove to them you have some courage—you will tell them the story of this poor devil who drowned in the Isere—and that you saved—

SIMPLICE: What! You remember it—

MARCELINE: Yes, I remember it! Didn't you give me as a fiancée bouquet, those beautiful beribboned flowers that this man delivered to you saying: this will bring you luck!

SIMPLICE: And you kept them?

MARCELINE: They are upstairs in my room, and you will see them on my bodice the day when you become completely brave.

SIMPLICE: Oh! Really! Don't worry! If that's what you need, you are going to see. (*going to the window*) There they are: let's escape!

MARCELINE: Ah! I will embolden you despite yourself. (*she escapes and locks the door*)

SIMPLICE: Hola! Marceline! They're here! I'm dead! (*hiding behind an empty wine cask*)

LANDRY: Long live old wine!

GUERFROID: Long live young girls!

LANDRY: The sight of bottles
　　Fills our hearts with joy!

GUERFROID: The sight of red lips
　　Works even better

LANDRY: *(spoken)* Heyo! Colleague!

GUERFROID: *(spoken)* Heyo! Companion! Heyo!

TOGETHER: Tick, tock! Mug against mug! Tick, tock! What a
　　happy shock! Straight as a rock! Proud as a cock! Let's drink in
　　block the whole wine cellar! And if someone unwisely braves
　　and defies us, let's beat him from head to toe!

*(They rap the boards with their hobnailed canes. Simplice is hiding
in the cask.)*

GUERFROID: Oh, the good life!
　　Gay and hearty fellows,
　　Shepherds and winegrowers,
　　Our fate is worthy of envy.
　　Oh, the good life!
　　Strong, young and handsome,
　　Winegrowers and shepherds
　　Our fate is worthy of envy.
　　They have to see us set the fashion
　　For the guys' assembly
　　We fight and twirl the baton
　　In the midst of melees.
　　To laugh, to sing, morning and night,
　　And all week, too
　　Good God! Colleague, they have to see us!
　　We're worth the trouble!

LANDRY: Well! They will see us
　　Always on holiday!
　　They will hear us
　　Repeat with all of our might:
　　Wine's a gift from the gods!

GUERFROID: Love is the pleasure of the gods.

LANDRY: Good wine that sparkles
Rejoices the eyes!

GUERFROID: A pretty girl
Does more for me!

LANDRY: *(spoken)* Ohey! Colleague.

GUERFROID: Ohey! Companion, ohey!

TOGETHER: Clink! Clank! Glass against glass! Clink! Clank! What a joyful shock! Straight like a rock! Proud like a cock! Let's drink in block the entire wine cellar! And if some fool braves and defies us, we'll beat him from head to toe! Clink! Clank! Glass against glass! Clink! Clank! What a joyful shock! Straight like a rock! Proud like a cock!

LANDRY: *(rapping on the table, spoken)* Hola! Hey! Papa Boniface!

GUERFROID: Hola!

BONIFACE: *(coming from the cellar)* Here! Here!

LANDRY: Hurry up, slow poke!

GUERFROID: Make it snappy!

BONIFACE: *(placing the mugs on the table)* There! There!

GUERFROID: How's your wife?

BONIFACE: My wife?

LANDRY: She's still young?

BONIFACE: Young—meaning—young—if you like.

GUERFROID: *(rapping the table)* We want to know if she's young?

BONIFACE: *(altered)* She is young!

LANDRY: And your daughter, Marceline? Pretty? Is she still pretty?

BONIFACE: My daughter Marceline! Pretty—if you like.

LANDRY: *(rapping the table)* We want to know if she's pretty!

BONIFACE: She is very pretty!

GUERFROID: On that note, busy yourself with supper, and take care that no one come to disturb us, or we will trim his ears.

SIMPLICE: *(aside)* I am dead!

LANDRY: What's that noise?

GUERFROID: Someone spoke.

BONIFACE: It was the rats!

LANDRY: Get going, scamper off.

BONIFACE: Right! *(he leaves by the left)*

GUERFROID: The country was good, colleague!

LANDRY: We are not returning empty hearted, companion! *(Simplice peeps out)* And what we did with those victims!

GUERFROID: Did we ever murder those dandies from the Midi! *(Simplice hides himself)* You know quite well that ten fine stout lads from Arles or Tarascon wouldn't frighten you, Landry!

(Simplice shows his head.)

LANDRY: You know, Guerfroid that fifteen blokes from Provence or the Carmogue wouldn't make you flinch.

GUERFROID: Well said. *(he chugalugs his entire mug)*

LANDRY: Well drunk!

GUERFROID: *(elbowing him)* Say, Landry?

LANDRY: Huh, Guerfroid?

GUERFROID: Do you understand?

LANDRY: I understand you well enough!

GUERFROID: Did we come here, in advance, to rest?

LANDRY: Are we going to only sleep and drink while waiting for the others?

SIMPLICE: *(aside)* What do they mean?

GUERFROID: *(pulling Landry aside)* The Dame Boniface—did you notice her?

LANDRY: Less than you, colleague!

GUERFROID: A well shaped woman! And who has got arms! And shoulders!

LANDRY: Keep going!

SIMPLICE: *(aside)* Poor Boniface!

GUERFROID: It's true she won't listen to any joking and that her imbecile of a husband never takes his eye off her, but we will find a way to get her away from him.

LANDRY: Well said! *(he drinks)*

GUERFROID: Well drunk!

LANDRY: *(pulling Guerfroid aside)* In your turn, Guerfroid, didn't you see trotting around the house a tender shoot of a girl, the sight of her alone puts you in good humor?

SIMPLICE: What's he saying?

GUERFROID: The daughter of Old Man Boniface!

SIMPLICE: *(loud)* Marceline!

GUERFROID What's that—?

LANDRY: Huh?

(Simplice rolls with his cask.)

TRIO:

GUERFROID:	LANDRY:	SIMPLICE:
Who goes there?	Stop there!	Hey, there!

TOGETHER:

GUERFROID AND LANDRY:
May the plague get him!
He heard everything!
We'll force him to shut up
Or indeed all is lost.
Let's break something of his,
Ribs, legs or arms,
For fear he'll cause us
Some new trouble.
If he comes, this devil of a man,
To discover our secrets,
First of all let's kill him,
And we'll worry about it later!

SIMPLICE:
Ah! Against their rage
Can I be protected?
The more I consider.
The more I see I am lost!
Oh, the terrible thing.
Oh, what a scrape,
And what horror
The fear of death is causing me!
Before they murder me
With blows with sticks
If I can do it — watch
Watch how I'll get away!

LANDRY: Look us in the face!

SIMPLICE: Mercy! Mercy!

GUERFROID: Where'd you get this audacity?

SIMPLICE: Terror is freezing me!

LANDRY: What new sort of wine
  Is escaping from its cask?

SIMPLICE: Mercy! Mercy!

GUERFROID: No grimaces
  Or I will smash you
  Into twenty pieces!

SIMPLICE: *(stumbling)* Cursed casks!

REPRISE:

GUERFROID AND LANDRY:
May the plague get him!
He heard everything!
We'll force him to shut up
Or indeed all is lost.
Let's break something of his,
Ribs, legs or arms,
For fear he'll cause us
Some new trouble.
If he comes, this devil of a man,
To discover our secrets,
First of all let's kill him,
And we'll worry about it later!

SIMPLICE:
Ah! Against their rage
Can I be protected?
The more I consider.
The more I see I am lost!
Oh, the terrible thing.
Oh, what a scrape,
And what horror they're causing me
The fear of death
Before they've murdered me
With blows with sticks
If I can do it like—
Like—I am going!

LANDRY: Answer frankly, or watch out!

SIMPLICE: I was strolling and by inadvertence
I fell into this cask.

LANDRY AND GUERFROID: Who are you, vile feather-brain?
Answer frankly, or beware!

SIMPLICE: I am the ferryman
Of the Isere ferryboat.
And I'll never ferry anymore
If you don't be nice!
I am the ferryman
Of the Isere ferryboat.

GUERFROID: Then what!
What were you doing there
In the bottom of this barrel?

SIMPLICE: Alas! Nothing worth mentioning!
I was closing my eyes and my ears
To rest them.

LANDRY: No, no, you lie!

GUERFROID: Bad luck to the traitor!

SIMPLICE: Who, me? You must know me—
I am the ferryman
Of the Isere ferryboat.
And I'll never ferry anymore
If you don't be nice.
I am the ferryman
Of the Isere ferryboat.

LANDRY: And what do you want, ferryman?

SIMPLICE: *(aside, hesitating)* Come on, courage! *(aloud)* I claim
the honor
Of entering into your company!

GUERFROID AND LANDRY: Ha! Ha! Ha!
Nice companion he'd make!

TOGETHER:

LANDRY, GUERFROID:	**SIMPLICE:**
He amuses me, he amuses me,	Let's escape by trickery
The poor lad!	From blows with the stick!
What a confused expression	So long as it abuses them,
For a companion!	All means are good!

GUERFROID: But to join us, do you know how to drink?

SIMPLICE: No question, much and fast!

LANDRY: You intend to make us believe it?

SIMPLICE: I'll drink the ocean in a gulp.

GUERFROID: *(laughing)* What! In a single gulp!

SIMPLICE: Yes, in a single gulp!

LANDRY: *(aside to Guerfroid)* He must drink, let him be drunk.
He can be useful to us today!

SIMPLICE: At least, they're letting me live!

LANDRY: But do you know how to make love?
And to fight
Like the devil himself?

SIMPLICE: *(after having drunk again)*
I'll lick
And I'll love
The whole world
In one round.
Yes, I'll love the whole world.

GUERFROID: Well! First off, we'll test you
And then, we will see!

LANDRY AND GUERFROID: Ha! Ha! Ha!
Nice companion he'd make!

TOGETHER:

LANDRY AND GUERFROID:	**SIMPLICE:**
He amuses me, he amuses me!	Let's escape through trickery
The poor boy,	From blows with a stick!
What a confused expression	So long as it abuses them
For a companion.	All means are good!

ALL THREE: We will drink. We'll laugh, We'll fight, We'll love, And we'll live As good jolly fellows!

LANDRY, GUERFROID AND SIMPLICE: Hey! Hey! Old Man Boniface! Hola!

(Enter Boniface holding two mugs which he places on the table. He is followed by two valets bringing supper.)

BONIFACE: Here! Here! *(noticing Simplice)* This cursed boatman again!

LANDRY: He's one of us *(he says some words into the ear of his valets)* You understand? *(the valet leaves)*

GUERFROID: *(to Boniface, pointing to Simplice)* He's the one's going to regale us this evening!

SIMPLICE: *(aside)* If I knew how, I would pay!

BONIFACE: Then he's come into an inheritance.

GUERFROID: Yes, he inherited from his aunt.

SIMPLICE: From my aunt!

BONIFACE: His aunt! Why she just remarried for the fourth time.

LANDRY: *(patting Simplice on the shoulder)* That's not all! *(turning to Boniface)* This dear friend was polite enough to invite your wife and daughter to share this supper with us.

SIMPLICE: *(aside)* Ah! My God!

GUERFROID: Aren't they hungry?

BONIFACE: They are hungry—if you like!

LANDRY: We want them to be hungry!

BONIFACE: They are dying of hunger.

GUERFROID: Start serving!

BONIFACE: *(to the waiters)* Serve!

GUERFROID: Here are the ladies.

BONIFACE: What do you mean?

GUERFROID: I sent Andeol to warn them.

(Monique and Marceline appear in the doorway. Andeol precedes them. Music from the orchestra.)

GUERFROID: Come in, ladies.

LANDRY: And deign to accept a place at our supper!

SIMPLICE: *(aside)* I'm not even the one who had the pleasure of inviting them.

GUERFROID: *(to Monique)* Dame Monique.

LANDRY: *(to Marceline)* Miss Marceline.

(Each takes a place at the table. Simplice finds himself seated between Guerfroid and Marceline. Marceline is near Landry, Monique by Guerfroid. The music continues.)

BONIFACE: *(who has vainly tried to place himself)* Hey! Why, I don't see any place for me.

LANDRY: Come on, Boniface, some action! Make the plates circulate. Fill the cups. Raise the napkins!

BONIFACE: But—why—

LANDRY: To the health of Marceline!

GUERFROID: To the health of Dame Monique *(Guerfroid tries to embrace Monique)*

MONIQUE: *(pushing him off)* Watch out for a slap!

SIMPLICE: My word! Let's drink to have courage.

GUERFROID: Wine, Boniface, wine!

BONIFACE: Here!

LANDRY: *(to Marceline)* And you, my pretty, a song!

SIMPLICE: A pretty roundelay, miss.

ALL: Yes! A roundelay.

MARCELINE: *(rising)* Here goes! *(singing)* At the market in
    Beaucaire,
    We go there twice a year,
    The girls wearing plain skirts,
    The lads in white hats.
    How noisy! How many people!
    They laugh, they dance in a circle
    And that's why,
    For business,
    We go there twice a year.
    To the market at Beaucaire!
    They sell everything there at high price
    And the affluence is great!
    More than one customer is taken
    By the pretty eyes of a salesgirl,
    And asks her
    If her heart is included
    In the objects she is selling.
    The beauty replies in whisper
    What's given's not for sale!
    At the market in Beaucaire,
    We go there twice a year,
    The girls wearing plain skirts,
    The lads in white hats.
    How noisy! How many people!
    They laugh, they dance in a circle
    And that's why,
    For business,
    We go there twice a year.

ALL: At the market in Beaucaire,
    We go there twice a year,
    The girls wearing plain skirts,
    The lads in white hats.
    How noisy! How many people!
    They laugh, they dance in a circle
    And that's why,

For business,
We go there twice a year.

MARCELINE: But if, surprised in its turn,
    When love entices it
    The heart flees without return
    From the bodice of the salesgirl.
    Like contraband
    They sign the deed
    When the beauty demands it.
    In all faith and honor
    Her hand goes to retrieve his heart!
    At the market in Beaucaire,
    We go there twice a year,
    The girls wearing plain skirts,
    The lads in white hats.
    How noisy! How many people!
    They laugh, they dance in a circle
    And that's why,
    For business,
    We go there twice a year.

ALL: At the market in Beaucaire, etc.
    We go there twice a year,
    The girls wearing plain skirts,
    The lads in white hats.
    How noisy! How many people!
    They laugh, they dance in a circle
    And that's why,
    For business,
    We go there twice a year.

(They rise and dance around the table.)

LANDRY: *(to Marceline)* Marceline— *(whispers to her)*

MARCELINE: *(moving away)* Your servant!

GUERFROID: *(to Monique)* Charming Monique! *(he kisses her)*

MONIQUE: *(whacking him)* Goodnight!

GUERFROID: Now there's a slap that Boniface will pay me for!

(The two women escape and leave.)

LANDRY: *(to Simplice)* Keep Boniface busy. *(to Guerfroid)* The husband mustn't see any more of this.

(Landry and Guerfroid leave by the back. Night begins to come on.)

SIMPLICE: Now they've left! I'd really like to go to sleep too.

BONIFACE: *(emptying the bottles)* Hey! Hey! My wine is fine!

SIMPLICE: *(aside)* My head is swimming! Why did they tell me to keep Boniface busy?

BONIFACE: *(singing and dancing at the same time)*
To the faire at Beaucaire
We go there twice a year,
The girls wearing plain skirts,
The lads in white hats.
How noisy! How many people!
They laugh, they dance in a circle
And that's why,
For business,
We go there twice a year.

SIMPLICE: Good night, Boniface!

BONIFACE: Heavens! The Boatman! Ah! Ah! Ah! You're not leaving my boy! You're not leaving! Why do you want to go?

SIMPLICE: I'm going to go to bed.

BONIFACE: *(retaining him)* Not at all!

SIMPLICE: I think I've drunk too much!

BONIFACE: Ah, bah! Since you're an heir—one doesn't inherit every day! Ah! Ah! Ah!

SIMPLICE: Until tomorrow, Papa Boniface, until tomorrow!

BONIFACE: *(retaining him)* Wait up. And we'll settle up. It's a question of doing our bill. You don't leave without paying!

SIMPLICE: What's he saying?

BONIFACE: I say you must pay.

SIMPLICE: But—but—I don't have a wooden nickel to give you! They were making fun of you, Papa Boniface. They were making fun of you! Ask the companions to pay! Me, I've got nothing!

BONIFACE: *(holding him by the neck)* Ah! That's the way it is.

SIMPLICE: So, there you are informed! Goodnight!

BONIFACE: One moment, I'm not releasing you.

SIMPLICE: But, since I haven't a sou altogether.

BONIFACE: *(taking him by the collar)* You won't leave!

MONIQUE: *(screaming outside)* Ah! Rogue! Good-for-nothing!

BONIFACE: *(releasing Simplice)* That's my wife's voice.

SIMPLICE: *(aside)* And Landry's instruction!

BONIFACE: Let's run, great god!

SIMPLICE: *(stopping him and grabbing him by the fist)* In your turn, you won't leave.

BONIFACE: Let me go, Simplice; there's something going on with my wife!

SIMPLICE: Heavens! But I've got a solid fist!

BONIFACE: Let's go! This is not the time to joke!

SIMPLICE: I'm not joking—I'm exercising to become strong!

MONIQUE: *(outside)* Boniface! Boniface!

BONIFACE: Are you going to release me?

SIMPLICE: Why, here, I have pity on you.

BONIFACE: *(disappearing through the door on the right)* Here I am, Monique!

SIMPLICE: *(alone)* Heavens! *(astonished)* I'm stronger than I would ever have thought. I have a solid fist when I want it. Ah! Ah! Ah! That poor Boniface. Is it this wine I drank that's giving me courage? Why, no! I recall what Marceline said to me. To be worthy of her I feel myself capable of facing all these Knights of the Daffodil! Marceline! Darling Marceline!

LANDRY: *(entering)* Marceline!

SIMPLICE: Huh?

LANDRY: May the devil take her! I waited an hour for her under the trees; the little idiot didn't come.

SIMPLICE: *(aside)* Ha!

LANDRY: I fear that poor Guerfroid hasn't been any luckier than me.

SIMPLICE: Ah! Ah!

LANDRY: For I saw the husband running with his valets armed with pitchforks—he had only time to jump out the window or risk falling again into the Isere. And this time he would really have been able to stay there. One doesn't always find an imbecile who's devoted enough to save him.

SIMPLICE: Ah, bah! *(aside)* Heavens—it was him!

LANDRY: *(pulling him aside)* Listen.

SIMPLICE: What is it?

LANDRY: I've one hope remaining.

SIMPLICE: What is it?

LANDRY: We are going to pretend to leave, Marceline is going to go to church for the angelus.

SIMPLICE: Yes—like every night with Dame Monique.

LANDRY: We will post ourselves in the shadows, we will carry the two of them off—we will transport them in your boat and we will take them to the other shore.

SIMPLICE: To the other shore!

LANDRY: Do you understand?

SIMPLICE: Yes—-yes—the angelus to the other shore—that's understood!

LANDRY: Offer to accompany her to the church—bring her to me, and by Jove—you will be one of us! *(heading toward the door)*

SIMPLICE: *(retaining him)* One moment!

LANDRY: What?

SIMPLICE: It's not going to happen!

LANDRY: Huh?

SIMPLICE: *(going for his throat)* I forbid you to do it!

LANDRY: What's wrong with him?

SIMPLICE: I want to kill you!

LANDRY: You?

SIMPLICE: Yes, me!

LANDRY: Are you crazy?

SIMPLICE: I'm in love with Marceline, that's all.

(The angelus can be heard,)

LANDRY: Ah, bah!

SIMPLICE: And I will prevent you from kidnapping her!

LANDRY: Ah! Ah! We are going to see!

SIMPLICE: What are we going to see?

GUERFROID: *(entering)* Ah! Bad kid—you let the husband escape!

SIMPLICE: Yes,—and I did it deliberately.

LANDRY: And he's refusing to help me because he loves Marceline.

SIMPLICE: Rather die a thousand times!

GUERFROID: In that case his account is going to be paid in full?

SIMPLICE: As will yours!

GUERFROID: Then you want to taste it, my little fellow.

SIMPLICE: As you say, my big boy!

LANDRY: You want to play with the stick!

SIMPLICE: Whenever you like, kids.

GUERFROID: Right away if it doesn't displease you too much.

SIMPLICE: En garde, then, because nothing is more agreeable to me.

GUERFROID: One moment! Let's do this by the rules, because the thing is serious. *(he takes off his hat and coat and secures a stick in his hand)* Hold yourself on the side, Landry, you are going to judge the hits. *(low)* He's going to ask mercy of me, he's going to see how I act.

(Guerfroid gives the customary bow and goes on guard.)

SIMPLICE: *(trying vainly to imitate him)* I don't know all your thrusts, but I'm going to play well and with good money. *(he seizes his oar and rushes on Guerfroid)*

(Boniface, Marceline and Monique enter with torches that light up the stage.)

FINAL SONG:

MONIQUE: Hey! What a row!
Peace!
Calm down!
See what rage!
Those guys are crazy.

LANDRY AND GUERFROID: *(rushing on Simplice)* No, we are fighting.
Watch out for the blows!

SIMPLICE: Watch out for the blows!

MONIQUE, BONIFACE: You are crazy.
Listen to us!

GUERFROID: No, no mercy! No mercy!
   Let's avenge ourselves, friend, let's avenge ourselves.

BONIFACE: *(restraining Simplice)* Peace, hey, peace!

MARCELINE: *(running in)* At your knees,
   For my spouse
   It's I that ask mercy!

LANDRY AND GUERFROID: Him! Your spouse?
   Can you think it!

MARCELINE: Since at last I am sure of your courage,
   Look at this withered bouquet,
   All beribboned,
   That I've pinned to my corsage. *(holding her hand to Simplice)*
   It's my marriage bouquet!

GUERFROID: That bouquet!

MARCELINE: Well!

GUERFROID: I recognize it! It's mine.

ALL: His!

GUERFROID: It was shipwrecked with me on the Isere one night.

MARCELINE: *(pointing to Simplice)* And he's the one who fished
   you out of the water!

GUERFROID: What!

LANDRY, MONIQUE, BONIFACE: You!

SIMPLICE: Me!

LANDRY AND GUERFROID: It's incredible!
   It's unheard of!
   What! It was him!
   The poor devil!
   What! It was him!

MARCELINE: Yes!
   It was him!

ALL: It was him!

GUERFROID: Well! In that case, my boy—put it there! *(offering his hand)*

SIMPLICE: With all my heart!

LANDRY: I'm interested in your luck. *(turning towards Boniface)* *(speaking)* Then, she's your wife. *(pushing Simplice into Marceline's arms)*

BONIFACE: *(speaking)* His wife? If you like!

GUERFROID: *(threatening him)* We want her to be his wife!

LANDRY, GUERFROID: But listen—down there—down there. Don't you hear?
Those are our friends coming to meet us!
Let's not make them wait!

SIMPLICE, MARCELINE, MONIQUE, BONIFACE: *(aside)* Thank god!
They're going to get out of here!

GUERFROID: *(to Boniface)* No hard feelings!

LANDRY: *(to Simplice)* No hard feelings!

GUERFROID, LANDRY: Come on, let's go to seek fortune. *(to Simplice)* You will be sacred to us.

LANDRY: But henceforth, bad luck to all!
Excepting you!

TOGETHER:

LANDRY AND GUERFROID:
Against all we are linked,
Knights of the Daffodil!
Against all we are linked,
Under the watch!

BONIFACE, MONIQUE, SIMPLICE, MARCELINE:
Against you, the watchful eye,
Knights of the Daffodil!
Against you, the watchful eye
Will be linked!

Curtain

MR. CHIMPANZEE

The giant prehistoric man in *Journey to the Center of the Earth.*

The human-like behavior of Jup the orang in *The Mysterious Island.*

M onsieur de Chimpanzé (*Mr. Chimpanzee*) was an operetta in one act, written by Verne with Michel Carré, and with music by Aristide Hignard. It was typical, in form and spirit, of the many opera-comiques that made the reputation of the Bouffes-Parisiens, a small Parisian theater managed by Jacques Offenbach. *Mr. Chimpanzee* was brought to the stage there on February 17, 1858 with a dozen performances following, and three were in 1859.

Like Verne's play *Voyage à travers l'impossible* (*Journey Through the Impossible*, 1882, published by the North American Jules Verne Society through Prometheus in 2003), *Mr. Chimpanzee* was considered lost for more than a century. At last, in 1978, both plays were discovered at the Archives nationales de Paris, in the archive of the Censorship Office of the Third French Republic. *Monsieur de Chimpanzé* was published in the *Bulletin de la Société Jules Verne*, no. 57 (1981). On November 4, 2005, *Monsieur de Chimpanzé* returned to the stage, at the Opéra de Metz, a city of Lorraine, France. The music is still lost, so a new score was written by Jean-Christophe Keck, an Offenbach specialist. Another version was presented at the University of Coimbra, Portugal, September 25, 2009, as part of the Researchers' Night with linked activities in a number of European cities and published in 2010.

By the time Verne authored *Mr. Chimpanzee*, he had placed two important novelettes in *Musée des Familles* (*Family Museum*), that also indicated future directions in his writing. *Maître Zacharius* (*Master Zacharius*) told how a watchmaker is tempted by the devil, and was published in April 1854. *Un hivernage dans les glaces* (*A Winter Amid the Ice*) was serialized in April and May of 1855, and related the fate of an Arctic expedition. (Both were translated into English in 1874.) *A Winter Amid the Ice* particularly presaged such polar stories as *Voyages et Aventures du capitaine Hatteras* (*Journeys and Adventures of Captain Hatteras*, 1866), *Le Pays des fourrures* (*The Fur Country*, 1873) and *Le Sphinx des Glaces* (*The Sphinx of the Ice*, 1897).

Of the four plays presented in this volume, *Mr. Chimpanzee* has the most in common with Verne's prose fiction, indicating themes he would follow in his "Voyages Extraordinaires" ("Extraordinary Journeys"). Composed long before he ever imagined becoming an author of science fiction, *Mr. Chimpanzee* nonetheless set the pattern of how Verne approached evolution and humankind's relationship with the ape. He called the play a "singerie musicale," or "musical monkey business." Most startling is that his fascination with the idea predates the November 24, 1859 publication of Charles Darwin's *On the Origin of Species by Means of Natural Selection, or the Preservation of Favoured Races in the Struggle for Life*. In France, Darwin's ideas were not popularized and seriously discussed until 1871. Nonetheless, it is impossible to read *Mr. Chimpanzee* today outside of the Darwinian prism.

Mr. Chimpanzee is another link for English language readers in Verne's treatment of humans, apes, and evolution. Here the question is placed in the framework of a musical comedy. Isidore, rejected by Van Carcass, the scientist father of his beloved, adopts a simian disguise to enter the savant's household and be near his sweetheart. Van Carcass shows little understanding of the apes he studies, and not until he proposes to dissect the creature is the disguise revealed. To prevent the couple from revealing how easily the scientist had been duped, he must agree to their wedding.

Is the monkey, in the words of the chorus, a brute or majestic beast? The failed servant Baptiste is less human and more foolish than Isidore, even when Isidore is still wearing his mask and speaking gibberish. After Baptiste is made valet to M. de Chimpanzee, in disguise, the ape proves to have better table manners than the servant. To Verne, not only is the ape part human, but some of the humans closely resemble apes. In *Voyage au centre de la Terre* (*Journey to the Center of the Earth*, 1864), a dream-like episode shows the discovery of a giant prehistoric man shepherding a herd of mastodons. *L'Île mystérieuse* (*The Mysterious Island*, 1875) inverts this idea, with a wild orangutan adopted into the family of the castaways, soon instinctively learning to smoke a pipe and even helping with the cooking.

While Verne was ostensibly an obedient Catholic, he never allowed the church's teachings to dissuade him from plots and characters foreign to Catholicism or even general Christian belief. His scientific bent fomented interest in thinking about the parallels between human and ape discussed by many at the time. Several other stories making this theme even more central did not appear in English until well into the 20th century.

An apparent relation of the giant prehistoric man in *Journey to the Center of the Earth* is purportedly uncovered in "Le Humbug" ("The Humbug," probably written in the 1860s, but only published in 1910). A huckster, Meade Augustus Hopkins, similar to P.T. Barnum, claims to have unearthed in upstate New York the bones of a 120 foot tall "missing link." The inspiration for the characterization and setting of "The Humbug" indicates the combination of hokum and science that were part of the 19th century discussions of evolution. The name of Verne's protagonist, Meade Augustus Hopkins, was originally Charles Vincent N_____ (the rest of the name has been crossed out and is no longer legible), perhaps in homage to the noted painter Charles Wilson Peale. Peale, who held what was regarded as the eccentric belief that humans had a relationship to the monkeys, was involved with excavations of prehistoric sites in the United States. The bones unearthed, including the first mastodon skeleton ever assembled, were displayed in the carnival-like atmosphere of his natural history museum in Philadelphia. Peale was not alone; Henry Augustus Ward was a collector for natural history museums, who had a successful business selling and exhibiting prehistoric bones, and his family said he met Verne in Paris.

Verne's 1887 short story, "Gil Braltar," simultaneously parodies humanity's similarity with the ape and British imperialism. "Gil Braltar" relates a near-successful invasion of Gibraltar, led by a mad Spanish hermit, the title character, who believes his name has destined him to free the island. As Gil Braltar demands the British surrender, Verne abruptly reveals that his army is a band of wild apes who have learned military maneuvers. A humiliating defeat on a key outpost of the empire is forestalled by the quick thinking of the British commander,

General MacKackmale (a pun on the name of the species of ape which still inhabits Gibraltar), whose hirsute and ugly appearance allows him to trick the apes by clothing himself in the hermit's furs and leading them back to the hills.

Verne introduces both Gil Braltar and MacKackmale with an animalistic description, noting that the general is a bit of a monkey, although nonetheless an excellent soldier. Ironically, the British stronghold is not threatened by the troops of any other country, and the attack is only repulsed when the garrison begin to act like apes themselves. Henceforth, Verne notes, to insure that any future simian invasion may be defeated by the same tactic, England will only send its most apelike officers to Gibraltar. In a further twist, Barnum exhibits the captured hermit, not as the man who nearly conquered Gibraltar, but as the Englishman who saved the fort!

Verne's literary penchant for simultaneously satirizing as well as acknowledging the importance of evolution is best exemplified in *Aventures de la famille Raton* (*Adventures of the Rat Family*, 1891). Using the style of Swift's *Gulliver's Travels* (1726), *Adventures of the Rat Family* is both a children's fairy tale and a parody. A close-knit family of rats is whimsically portrayed as magically transformed into various forms of life, moving up and down the evolutionary ladder. Their amusing incarnations include various lower forms, from mollusks to birds, finally rising from the lowliest species to make a metamorphosis into humankind.

An evil magician has interefered with the evolution of *The Rat Family*, leaving one a donkey, in Verne's 1891 fairty tale.

Verne well knew that the presentation of a serious idea—the similarity between human and ape and the essential truth

A missing link is discovered in *The Aerial Village*.

of evolution—could best be presented to an audience in an indirect form. As an author of nuance and subtlety, Verne frequently masked the important themes of his books within traditional narrative conventions. Hence, *Adventures of the Rat Family* echoes the light-hearted, musical comedy tone already used to approach the subject in *Mr. Chimpanzee*, "The Humbug," and "Gil Braltar."

However, Verne's treatment of evolution was not always humorous. *Le Village aérien* (*The Aerial Village*, 1901) depicts a race of ape-men, although Verne disingenuously announced that the book should not be interpreted as an endorsement of Darwin, and discreetly chose the formula of a jungle adventure. The survivors of a lost safari try to return to civilization, but actually move steadily back toward a more primitive state as they travel into an ever more mysterious, uncharted netherworld. Despite a shortage of food, they realize their increasing oneness with the wilds, and refuse to eat monkeys, believing it to be a form of cannibalism. Their journey is a transition carrying them from their own world to the city of a missing link between human and ape, a type of Java man. The tribe, who have their own language and call themselves the Waggdis, have permanent families and an organized town located in the trees of a giant forest. They evidence what Verne seems to believe is the uniquely human trait, religion, and have their own pope, Dr. Johausen, a mad European who, in attempting to study them, has reverted to a primitive state.

The idea of evolution and the kinship of human and ape deeply fascinated Verne throughout not only novels, but also short stories, a fairy tale, and a play. Readers can recognize the similarity in theme, narrative, and technique between the prose writer and the playwright.

CHARACTERS

VAN CARCASS, employed at the Museum of Rotterdam

ETAMINE, his daughter

BAPTISTE, his servant

ISIDORE, Called THE CHIMPANZEE

AT RISE, Baptiste is alone on the stage waxing the floor; proudly he interrupts his work and stands straight up.

BAPTISTE: What! To leave possibly one of the greatest families in Spain and to be reduced to entering the domestic service in the home of a museum curator! To descend from the Dukes of Las Pirouettas y Guimbardo y Tambour de Basco de la Cibouletta and to ceaselessly climb up to the top of a granary! To serve a man who lives in the midst of stuffed animals! Fatal destiny! Bitter scorn! *(he waxes, raging)* After that, Doctor Van Carcass, my master, has a very pretty daughter, Miss Etamine! Truly, beside her, the Queen would almost seem ugly! I love that young girl whose childhood was spent in the midst of animal skeletons of all sorts: why doesn't she love me? *(he clasps the mop to his breast)* Under this broom beats a manly heart? Yes! A warm heart beats! Meaning, no! A heart beats warmly! No. In the end, never mind! *(coming forward)* Ah! If I was in Spain, young girl, if I had a jerkin with sleeves like they have there. *(he points to his used smock coat)* If I wore the high breeches of my ancestors—I would sing you a serenade.

(Baptiste sings and accompanies himself with his broom.)

BAPTISTE: By Saint James of Compestella,

 I would say to you: Hey, beautiful,
 Come smoke a cigarette,
 Come with your caballero,

Come with me to Castilla!
Come where the Sherry sparkles,
Come to the palace of the Alcazar,
By our lady of El Pilar!
In your promenade
It's my serenade
Following your steps
Nothing can separate us.
My mad guitarre
Shivers down low!
Under your mantilla
Hide, young chica,
Your blond attractions,
And in the somber night
Listen in the shadows.
Don't you hear it?
By Saint James de Compestella
I would say to you: Hey, beautiful
Come smoke a cigarette,
Come with your caballero,
Come with me to Castilla!
Come where the Sherry sparkles,
Come to the palace of the Alcazar.
By our lady of El Pilar!
To you
To me! *(as he says these last words, he receives a violent kick,*
    he turns saying and singing)
To me! By our lady of El Pilar!

VAN CARCASS: I just put money in an envelope to throw in the street and it's you singing, Baptiste.

BAPTISTE: I'm humming, not to displease your honor.

VAN CARCASS: Did I take you into my service to hum: since when do my mops get transformed in your hands into Spanish mandolins?

BAPTISTE: Since the noble family de las Cabriolas della testa—

VAN CARCASS: Enough, Baptiste. I'm aware of your mania. You are not descended from anyone, your race begins with you; but I will have your name transmitted for future centuries throughout the world.

BAPTISTE: *(moved)* Thanks for that fine word, sir, thanks. *(shaking Van Carcass's hand)*

VAN CARCASS: *(prying his hand loose)* You know what I promised you. When your soul leaves this prison of a yellow vest with its horned buttons and green-smock coat with orange tassels, in other words when you accomplish the act of death, I promised you a favor which has, until now, been reserved for the great of the earth, and kings beneath their golden arches, a favor which will preserve you for the admiration of posterity more than all the glory of the Las Cabriolas. In a word I will stuff you, Baptiste!

BAPTISTE: Oh! Thanks for that fine word! Thanks. *(he shakes his hand again)*

VAN CARCASS: Take it easy! I will stuff you with vegetable fibers! I will place you in my museum between the Ichthyosaurus and the Megalatheurium and in a posture that will suit you!

BAPTISTE: *(posing)* Like this.

VAN CARCASS: Yes, but on the condition that you behave during your life, which we will shorten little by little in perfect domestic service. And, on that topic, I am expecting today a guest to whose service I am conditionally attaching you.

BAPTISTE: A new master to serve! And where will I have the time for it! Make me another arm!

VAN CARCASS: You're arguing, Baptiste! Be careful I don't stuff you with hay and old oakum.

BAPTISTE: *(furious)* Why not old rags that beggars put on!

VAN CARCASS: It will be put on, beware of doubting it, if—

BAPTISTE: Well, who are you waiting for?

VAN CARCASS: You will be very astonished, Baptiste, really stupefied, really speechless when I tell you who it is—but here's my daughter. *(enter Etamine)* Come closer, daughter, the pride of my museum; embrace your father, whose day today is one of the most beautiful days.

ETAMINE: You spent a good night?

VAN CARCASS: No, not good, but excellent; I dreamed of a monkey.

BAPTISTE: That means money!

VAN CARCASS: It means honor and glory!

BAPTISTE: *(considering Etamine)* Oh! I love her! I love her.

VAN CARCASS: What's gotten into you, Baptiste? This duster isn't a chicken needing its feathers plucked.

ETAMINE: Poor Baptiste, always the same, always idiotic.

BAPTISTE: Oh! Thanks for that kind word!

VAN CARCASS: And now Etamine, as you have sufficiently embraced your father, lend me an attentive ear.

ETAMINE: I'm listening to you.

VAN CARCASS: You know I've neglected nothing to make you happy; I've surrounded your childhood with the most interesting animals in creation, while waiting to find you a husband.

ETAMINE: Father, you know I love Mr. Isidore whom you won't receive!

VAN CARCASS: Isidore, the son of that dabbler in tulips from Rotterdam!

BAPTISTE: Never, miss! Never! The marriage cannot take place; it won't happen! By the Alhambra!

ETAMINE: Why's Baptiste meddling!

VAN CARCASS: Indeed, who asked your opinion? I find you very bold! If ever you permit yourself to give your opinion—after all, as it conforms to mine, I pardon you—

ETAMINE: Still!

VAN CARCASS: Never shall the daughter of a Van Carcass be the daughter-in-law of a tulip-tree whose collection attracts more tourists than my museum! To return to what I was saying, where was I, Baptiste?

BAPTISTE: While waiting to find you a husband.

VAN CARCASS: Ah! I've surrounded your childhood with the most interesting animals in creation while waiting to find you a husband. To complete my work I've addressed myself to correspondents in Brazil and I've received notice that one day very soon I will receive by steamboat—

BAPTISTE: The one who is as yet unknown. A spouse for Miss.

VAN CARCASS: A monkey of the largest type.

BAPTISTE: A monkey! You are giving her to a monkey!

ETAMINE: Never!

VAN CARCASS: Not a little mongrel of a monkey, a South American monkey, a marmoset, but the type that my natural history exhibit is lacking, a true man of the forests, the unique, the last of the chimpanzees.

BAPTISTE: A chimpanzee!

ETAMINE: And what are we going to do with this villainous beast?

BAPTISTE: And that's the being to which you are going to provisionally attach me?

VAN CARCASS: Don't be afraid, Baptiste! This animal isn't ferocious except when it reaches a ripe old age!

BAPTISTE: But the one you are expecting is young?

VAN CARCASS: Of that I am completely unaware!

BAPTISTE: Eh! Well! Thanks! A man of the woods, an orangutan.

VAN CARCASS: Where's this speech headed?

BAPTISTE: I positively refuse to have any relations with him.

VAN CARCASS: You don't have any common sense, Baptiste.

BAPTISTE: No, I have noble sense, and I am not made to be the valet de chamber of a Barbary ape!

VAN CARCASS: Take care! This monkey is becoming my guest, my boarder.

BAPTISTE: What, dirty, even very dirty.

VAN CARCASS: And I won't tolerate the laws of hospitality being violated in the home of Doctor Van Carcass.

(A ringing is heard.)

VAN CARCASS: See who that is?

ETAMINE: It's him without a doubt!

(A formidable shriek is heard.)

VAN CARCASS: I recognize his voice! Obey, Baptiste. *(Baptiste leaves, furious)* Be happy, daughter, this chimpanzee was lacking to the happiness and museum of your father.

(Two sailors carrying a huge sack; they open it and Isidore, covered with a monkey hide and a well adjusted mask, comes out triumphantly, with a terrible scream; Baptiste is tripped up, the sailors bow and leave.)

TOGETHER:

BAPTISTE:	VAN CARCASS:	ETAMINE:
Ah! What an animal	What a fine animal!	Ah! What an animal!
How brutish he is!	How colossal!	He seems brutal.
He will harm us!	How like a judge!	He's colossal
Ah! What an animal!	Ah! What an animal!	Ah! What an animal!

ISIDORE: *(yelling)* IRI CRIM INERI!

VAN CARCASS: Do you hear his scream!

BAPTISTE: I am completely confused!

ETAMINE: It's a horrible scream!

BAPTISTE: I'm completely confused.

ISIDORE: IRI CRIM INERI!

TOGETHER:

BAPTISTE:	VAN CARCASS:
Ah! What an animal!	What a fine animal!
How brutish he is!	How colossal!
He will harm us!	How like a judge!
Ah! What an animal!	Ah! What an animal!

VAN CARCASS: Isn't this the king of the forest!

BAPTISTE: A king of a horrifying race!

VAN CARCASS: Almost human!

BAPTISTE: How he grimaces and gesticulates!

VAN CARCASS: Observe this charming primitive! How well he stands for a monkey!

BAPTISTE: He's a man of the world, only lacking a fine lineage!

TOGETHER:

BAPTISTE:	VAN CARCASS:	ETAMINE:
Ah! What an animal!	The fine animal!	Ah! What an animal!
How brutish!	He's colossal!	He is colossal!
Ah! May the devil take him!	See how well he takes care of himself.	To present himself this way!
What a way he dresses!	What a proud face and bearing!	He must leave right away!
Ah! What an animal!	The fine animal!	Ah! What an animal!

VAN CARCASS: *(to the monkey)* Take it easy! Hey, there, my pretty.

ISIDORE: Incriminieri!

ETAMINE: Take care, father, he's going to bite you.

VAN CARCASS: No! It doesn't bite!

BAPTISTE: *(advancing his finger)* Let's see!

ISIDORE: *(rushing on him)* Ahi!

BAPTISTE: Yikes!

ISIDORE: Incriminieri!

BAPTISTE: What's that mean in monkey talk?

VAN CARCASS: No doubt it signifies he's hungry.

ETAMINE: What do these beasts eat, Papa?

BAPTISTE: I am allowed to say they swallow a little bit of everything, gloves, soles of shoes, the legs even, silk hats,—

VAN CARCASS: You are mistaken, Baptiste, those are ostriches. These monkeys are very fond of good things, of sweets. You are going to busy yourself with his meal!

BAPTISTE: Excuse me, Mr. Van Carcass, but I haven't eaten yet.

VAN CARCASS: Well! You will eat later!

BAPTISTE: After a monkey! That degrades me.

VAN CARCASS: Well! That will nourish you, did you believe that you were worth more than this noble animal? What have you got more than he has, if you please? Are you more elegant, better turned out, isn't he a true man, and who has the advantage over you of not saying stupidities? Didn't you read in Mr. Bouffon that these animals are susceptible to good things, that they can stand attendance, drink and eat like natural people! And that they don't exact wages for serving their master? The monkey is compared to a servant like a black slave to a white man: His equal, except for the color. Try not to forget it.

BAPTISTE: Oh! Humiliation! Degradation of the human species! Exploitation of man by monkey!

ETAMINE: On careful examination, he's not bad, this animal.

VAN CARCASS: Say, then, Etamine, how full he is of nobility and grace; he seems very well brought up! If he had gloves he would be received in the best houses!

BAPTISTE: On his feet and his hands!

ISIDORE: INCRIMINIERI!

VAN CARCASS: That's probably Brazilian! C'mon, baby, baby! Give me your paw! You're going to see.

BAPTISTE: Probably it's necessary to talk in pidgin to him, sir.

VAN CARCASS: You're right, Baptiste. Baby, gimme paw-paw!

(Isidore gives his leg.)

BAPTISTE: Oh-oh! He doesn't know the difference between his leg and his arm!

VAN CARCASS: Why, no! He's right! I asked him for his paw and he gave it to me. Ask him for his hand and you will see!

BAPTISTE: Baby, baby, gimme hand-hand! *(Isidore rakes his head with his claws)* Help! Help! Villainous beast!

VAN CARCASS: He is adorable! Baptiste, why didn't you ask for his hand in velvet!

BAPTISTE: It's an infamy!

ETAMINE: What shall we call him, papa?

VAN CARCASS: Etamine's right! We must find him a name.

BAPTISTE: Suppose we call him, Gonzalvo.

ETAMINE: Oh, no. That's not swanky enough.

VAN CARCASS: The fact is, he has a bearing that couldn't be more distinguished. Ah! I've got what we need! Mr. Chimpanzee.

BAPTISTE: A noble! Never!

VAN CARCASS: Oh! I am going to get annoyed in the end! Baptiste! You will call him Mr. Chimpanzee or we're going to quarrel! You will speak to him in the third person or I am going to kick you out.

ETAMINE: Goodbye, Mr. Chimpanzee.

VAN CARCASS: I am going to appear before the zoological society to share news of my acquisition! Prepare Mr. Chimpanzee's meal and have the care you ought for him and his species.

BAPTISTE: If Mr. Chimpanzee would kindly permit me, I am going to have the honor of bringing to Mr. Chimpanzee the meal I'll prepare with my own hands for Mr. Chimpanzee.

(All leave except Isidore.)

ISIDORE: *(alone)* Ouf! *(he takes off his mask furtively after first having made some ape like gambols)* I'm suffocating! How hot the apes must be! You see what love has reduced me to! To abdicate my dignity as a man! It seems to me that I am itching all over! Etamine! Etamine! At last I am going to speak to you and see you! Mr. Van Carcass had always shown me the door. Once I learned that he was expecting a monkey from Brazil, I didn't hesitate to dress in this chimpanzee outfit! But let's behave well and not be too nasty, for fear they'll chain us up! Let's have good manners to keep our freedom. Oof! It's not easy, in this thing! I don't know how the monkeys stand it.

RECITATIVE:

> Since I put on this macaque's skin,
> I feel like a hypochondriac!
> I no longer have human feelings
> And I feel myself sharpening my claws.
> Oh! Strange prodigy,
> My whole being is changing.
> Words in my throat take on another sound,
> And end, alas, in a frightful croak!
> I'm becoming a real monkey!
> It's no longer to be doubted!
> The thing is very strahaange!
> But if you could hear me,
> How my voice is chaanged
> I'm becoming a real monkey!
> I'm playing the man of the woods
> I think,
> And only for you, young girl
> A livery!
> In me you see a chimpanzee
> Slyly.

For this trick you must excuse me.
Oh! I love you.
But will you recognize me
For a fine young man?
My Etamine! See how
Briefly I am dressed!
I'm becoming a real monkey!
It's no longer to be doubted!
The thing is very strahaange!
But will you listen to me
Since my voice is chaanged!
I'm becoming a real monkey!
This lovely day, I intend
To astonish your praise—ah!
Look with love
And do not chaange!
One day we will share
Happiness unchaanged!
Love for your love,
My clever!
I'm becoming a real monkey!
It's no longer to be doubted!
The thing is very strahaange!
But will you listen
Now my voice is chaanged!

I'm becoming a real monkey. *(spoken)* Someone's coming! That Baptiste! Alert, let's conquer him, it won't be difficult to abuse him.

(Isidore takes the mop in one hand, and puts brushes on his feet and vigorously waxes the floor.)

BAPTISTE: *(bringing different foods)* I'm bringing my dinner at the same time as the Chimpanzee's! So what! What's he doing there. *(Isidore waxes with thousands of contortions and grimaces.)* He's waxing my floor! That's great! Why he does it marvelously well. Bravo, Mr. Chimpanzee. *(placing his foods on the buffet)*

ISIDORE: *(with a friendly manner)* IFPOINSIGHIGHI!

BAPTISTE: Yes, my friend, it's shining enough like that! But take care of getting tired.

ISIDORE: Shifissfiss fiss! *(he takes off the brushes and starts to sweep with a rare energy)*

BAPTISTE: Decidedly, this animal has served in the best homes in America. By the Escurial, here's an idea that's not beastly; I will make him do my work, and I will only have to cross my arms! If I had the carriage of my ancestors, I'd make him mount behind like a slave.

(Isidore comes sweeping right up to Baptiste's feet.)

BAPTISTE: Hey there. Let's take it easy, my friend. Take care of breaking the mirror.

(Isidore dusts the mirror, he dusts with the feather duster, then he opens the clock.)

BAPTISTE: Easy! Easy! Let's not joke with the big springs. Well! What's he doing?

(Isidore cleans the clock with an exquisite delicacy and imitates the grinding of the springs.)

ISIDORE: Crrrri! Crrrri! Crrri!

BAPTISTE: Crrri! Crrri! Now he's making me speak Dutch. Why he knows everything! He's truly a fashionable monkey! My word, the only thing left for me to do is eat.

ISIDORE: *(opening his mouth)* Am! Am! Am! Am!

BAPTISTE: You're hungry, my treasure! Don't worry! I've got the remainder of my old veal which will do for you.

(Isidore brings the table to the middle of the room and puts a napkin and place mats on it.)

BAPTISTE: Why he knows how to lay a table! Now there's a lad who'd have no trouble earning a hundred crowns a year, and even more if he were given a chance.

(Isidore brings a glass for Baptiste, he spits and dries it carefully with his napkin.)

BAPTISTE: Why he's of the latest type! He must have served in the homes of Princes!

(Isidore brings up a chair.)

BAPTISTE: My word, this is the first time I've been served at table! Why he must really be a descendant of Las Pirouettas.

ISIDORE: *(laughing)* Aeion! Aeion!

BAPTISTE: Why one would say he understands! This is prodigious! Now there's a character who can do everything.

ISIDORE: Am! Am! Am!

BAPTISTE: Yes, you're hungry! Because I understand you! Well, Mr. Chimpanzee, I want you to take a seat at my side.

(Isidore makes ceremonious manners.)

BAPTISTE: No, indeed, I tell you! I permit it!

(Isidore excuses himself better.)

BAPTISTE: Since I repeat to you that you would be pleasing me! Look, don't make me beg you!

(Isidore makes a sign that he would never dare.)

BAPTISTE: I wish it! Look! Do you want me to get annoyed at the end?

(Isidore finds a chair and sits near Baptiste.)

BAPTISTE: I am going to make him drink a little glass, and he will really enjoy it! Decidedly, he's a precious animal, I will make him my intimate friend.

(Isidore pours a drink for Baptiste after having uncorked a bottle and poured a few drops in his glass.)

BAPTISTE: He's amazing!

DUO:

BAPTISTE: *(drinking)*
>Hey, Mr. Chimpanzee,
>You are so civilized!
>Allow me to call you
>A gallant man!
>Thus I am honored
>To drink your health.

(They both drink, rise and click glasses.)

TOGETHER:

ISIDORE: *(aside)*	**BAPTISTE:**
Here my ruse	How useful he is!
In the end takes him in	Ah! How he amuses me!
And everything's going fine.	Why the way he drinks is very fine!
What an imbecile,	He's docile,
Easy tempered.	Easy tempered
Come, I fear nothing,	I'm no longer afraid,
Everything's fine!	Always fine!

BAPTISTE: Hey! How fine is this wine!

ISIDORE: Ah! Ah! Ah! Ah! Ah! Ah! Ah! Ah!

BAPTISTE: He never tasted any.

ISIDORE: Hey! Hey! Hey! Hey! Hey! Hey! Hey! Hey! Hey!

BAPTISTE: As for me, I love it when he drinks this way!

ISIDORE: Hi! Hi! Hi! Hi! Hi! Hi! Hi! Hi!

BAPTISTE: Elbows high and glasses high!

ISIDORE: Ho! Ho! Ho! Ho! Ho! Ho! Ho! Ho!

BAPTISTE: Ah! I have never drunk so much!

ISIDORE: Hu! Hu! Hu! Hu! Hu! Hu! Hu! Hu!

(They click and drink again.)

BAPTISTE: To your health!

ISIDORE: Hiricriminieri!

TOGETHER:

ISIDORE:	BAPTISTE:
Here my ruse	How useful he is!
In the end takes him in	Oh! How he amuses me!
And everything's going fine!	Why, he does drink well!
What an imbecile,	He's so docile,
With an easy temper.	With an easy temper.
Come, I fear nothing,	I'm no longer afraid.
Everything's going fine!	Never afraid again!

(Baptiste empties the bottle and becomes drunk little by little.)

ISIDORE: *(aside)* He's drunk now!

BAPTISTE: How interesting he is!

ISIDORE: He's starting to lose his head!

BAPTISTE: Give me a hand!

ISIDORE: Yezolechum!

BAPTISTE: You'd say he was speaking.

ISIDORE: Nahitzda wine!

BAPTISTE: Yez, it's the wine!

(Baptiste puts his arm around Chimpanzee.)

BAPTISTE: Friend, on my word,
　　I want to teach you
　　A Creole song.

ISIDORE: Zuitsme!

BAPTISTE: Here goes: *(singing)*
　　Coco zin zin!
　　La passio di zin zin,
　　Cocorico corico,
　　Gimme a drink.

(As Baptiste repeats the song, Isidore dances a roulade.)

BAPTISTE: You,
　　Sing with me!

BAPTISTE:	**ISIDORE:**
Coco zin zin!	Ah! Ah! Ah! Ah!
La passio di zin zin,	Ah! Ah! Ah! Ah! Ah!
Cocorico corico	Ah! Ah! Ah! Ah!
Gimme a drink!	Ah! Ah! Ah! Ah!

BAPTISTE: Ah! Me very happy!
  Chimpie you pleez me!

ISIDORE: Wannadoitagain?

BAPTISTE: Since you're here
  We'll dance the cha-cha!

(Isidore and Baptiste dance a black slave dance. Isidore performs the most hazardous cabrioles. He tosses chairs in the air, overturns the table, etc.)

TOGETHER:
  Tra, la, la, la, la.
  Let's dance the cha-cha.

(At the end, exhausted, Baptiste falls to the ground. Isidore fans him with his handkerchief. The door opens. Etamine rushes in over all this uproar.)

ETAMINE: What an uproar! What a brouhaha!

BAPTISTE: *(to Isidore)* Kiss me, my sweet friend!

ETAMINE: Well! Baptiste!

BAPTISTE: We are the best friends in the world!

ETAMINE: You are going to get yourself bit!

BAPTISTE: Him, bite me? Rather he will dine on me! I've never met a better bred man. See, Miss. *(Isidore picks up the table and brings a chair for Etamine.)* Could he be more gallant?

(Isidore offers his paw to Etamine.)

ETAMINE: *(frightened)* Oh!

BAPTISTE: Don't be afraid; I'm sure he's going to pay court to you.

ETAMINE: You're out of your mind, Baptiste.

BAPTISTE: *(with nobility)* By the castanets of my ancestors! Am I not here to defend you! Would I tolerate a clown to disrespect you! Etamine, Miss Etamine, doesn't my life belong to you?

ETAMINE: He's babbling! Here I am between a monkey and a madman!

BAPTISTE: My whole life is devoted to you! I don't give my broom a whisk without thinking of your beautiful little white hands! I don't wax a tile in the floor without thinking of your pretty Andalousian feet.

ISIDORE: *(aside)* Wait, wait! I've got a foot, too!

BAPTISTE: Oh! Young lady, I love you! How Gatilbaza loves Dona Etamine! Besides your dove like beauty! The King said it to his nephew! Dance peasants! The wind which blows across the mountain has blown me to Mount Falou!

ISIDORE: *(giving him a kick)* Here! He needs it!

BAPTISTE: Hey! *(new kick)* What's got in to him? It's a twitch! *(he runs around the room pursued by Isidore's kicks)* Enough! Enough! Damn! Double damn! Goddam! A descendant of Las—he's rabid!

(Isidore sends him into the wings with a final kick. Etamine bursts into loud laughter.)

ISIDORE: We are alone. *(he removes his mask)*

ETAMINE: What! It's you, Isidore! It's not a dream!

ISIDORE: *(taking her in his arms)* No, it's not a monkey! Here's the moment to sing a real duo in a comic opera situation.

DUO:

ETAMINE: It's really you!

ISIDORE: Yes, it's me!

TOGETHER:

ISIDORE:	ETAMINE:
Supreme moment,	Supreme moment,
Extreme joy.	Extreme joy.
The one I love	The one I love
Is near me.	Is near me.
O sweet intoxication!	O sweet intoxication!
Darling mistress,	I'm your mistress,
Yes, my tenderness	Whose tenderness
I'm all yours.	Is all yours.

ETAMINE: But they must hear us!

ISIDORE: Someone might surprise us
And separate us forever!

ETAMINE: *(with exaltation)* Heaven protect our love! *(spoken)*
Still—

TOGETHER:
Be prudent,
Sing lower.
Let silence be heard.
Don't speak,
Silence!

ETAMINE: God! If my father comes to discover us—how will you
be able to escape?

ISIDORE: By jumping out the window!

ETAMINE: You will break your neck!

ISIDORE: Come on! Am I not a chimpanzee! I cross the steepest
rocks, I scale the highest trees; I am susceptible to attachment,
I live in groups in the forest, and I have for my little ones a
particular affection—says Mr. de Bouffon.

ETAMINE: Poor Isidore! He finds a way to laugh under this garb.

ISIDORE: You forgive me, right, and you love me?

ETAMINE: Oh! Yes!

ISIDORE: A kiss for the trouble it cost me.

ETAMINE: Oh! Never!

ISIDORE: Suppose that I am a greyhound, a pretty tom-cat, nothing would prevent you from kissing me, from caressing me.

ETAMINE: Yes, but it's not the same thing.

ISIDORE: Think carefully, that if I hadn't put on this parakeet's skin I would never have been able to get in here.

(He kisses her.)

ETAMINE: Heavens! They're coming. Put on your muzzle!

(Isidore leaves and quickly returns with his masque.)

(Music)

BAPTISTE: *(off)* Don't go in! I tell you he's rabid!

VAN CARCASS: Out of the way, imbecile, and don't be afraid. I am armed.

(Van Carcass comes in passing in front of Baptiste.)

BAPTISTE: Oh!

ETAMINE: Father!

VAN CARCASS: My daughter! Just in time!

(Isidore shows his teeth to Baptiste who hides behind his master.)

BAPTISTE: Help!

VAN CARCASS: Hush! Don't budge! He's capable of jumping out of the window! And I don't want him to escape me.

ETAMINE: What's your plan, father?

VAN CARCASS: Hush! Since he's gone bad, and he's breaking my furniture, I've decided—

ETAMINE: To do what?

VAN CARCASS: *(pulling an enormous cutlass from his breast)* That he will become the most beautiful ornament in my museum. We are going to skin him right away!

ISIDORE: *(aside)* Skin me!

VAN CARCASS: We will stuff him afterwards.

BAPTISTE: But you were indifferent to stuffing him before.

VAN CARCASS: Imbecile!

BAPTISTE: Thanks for that nice word!

VAN CARCASS: Seize that animal.

BAPTISTE: *(terrified)* It's that—

ISIDORE: *(yelling)* DAMMIT!

VAN CARCASS: Come on, go take one arm—I will hold the other.

BAPTISTE: I'm holding one arm.

VAN CARCASS: And me the other.

(They lead Isidore to the middle of the room.)

BAPTISTE: Go!

ETAMINE: *(rushing between them)* Stop, father, I love him!

VAN CARCASS: Huh! You love him! Don't worry, Etamine, I will replace him with a more docile animal, a cat, a marmoset.

ETAMINE: No, father I love him—in love with him.

VAN CARCASS: In love! This monkey! Withdraw!

ETAMINE: Yes, in love!

ISIDORE: *(knocking Baptiste over)* Oh! Thanks, my God!

VAN CARCASS: *(stupefied)* Huh!

BAPTISTE: He's talking. A monkey genius!

ISIDORE: *(removing his mask)* No! Just your future son-in-law.

VAN CARCASS: Isidore! Beggar! *(raising his cutlass)*

ISIDORE: Marry us! Or I will tell everybody that a scientist like Doctor Van Carcass let himself be taken in by a monkey skin!

VAN CARCASS: The devil!

ISIDORE: And he'll become a public laughing stock.

VAN CARCASS: Enough! Enough! You disarm me. *(he lets his cutlass fall)* My daughter is yours!

ETAMINE: Ah, father!

ISIDORE: Etamine, in my paws—no! In my arms! Let's go to the registry.

VAN CARCASS: What are you thinking of doing? In that costume!

ISIDORE: I'll put on a white vest.

BAPTISTE: This marriage will never take place, sir. The Las Pirouettas—

ISIDORE: Here! Now there are some pirouettes.

(Isidore spins Baptiste around and gives him a kick in the ass. Baptiste falls back down.)

VAN CARCASS: But with all this, I no longer have a monkey! My daughter has fulfilled her wishes, but as for me—

ISIDORE: Take my skin, and be satisfied!

FINALE *(reprise of the Cha-cha theme)*
    Coco zin zin!
    La passio di zin zin,
    Cocorico corico,
    Gimme a drink.

BAPTISTE: *(on a tremolo from the orchestra)* Mr. Van Carcass?

VAN CARCASS: Baptiste!

BAPTISTE: How many ribs?

VAN CARCASS: Twelve, one in the other.

BAPTISTE: *(feeling)* I only feel seven—five have been crushed.

VAN CARCASS: Bah! I'll put them back for you in my spare time.

BAPTISTE: Thanks for that fine word! Bring on the Cha-cha.

REPRISE OF THE CHA-CHA:
Coco zin zin!
La passio di zin zin,
Cocorico corico,
Gimme a drink.

Curtain

THE ADOPTIVE SON

The theme of *The Adoptive Son*, trying to gain adoption through rescuing a wealthy man, reappears in *Clovis Dardentor* (1896).

The one-act comedy, *Un Fils adoptif* (*An Adopted Son*), was written by Verne with Charles Wallut around 1853. It was never staged, but the manuscript was known, and it was adapted for a radio broadcast on France-Inter on April 5, 1950. The original play was finally published in *Bulletin de la Société Jules Verne*, no. 140 (2000). This translation incorporates changes to the manuscript by Victorien Sardou.

An Adopted Son is part of a series of comedies where Verne and Wallut exploit the comedic possibilities of legal peculiarities of law, as in *Eleven Days of Siege* and *Un Neveu d'Amérique, ou, les deux Frontignac* (*An American Nephew, or, the Two Frontignacs*, 1861). In one passage there are also echoes of the humor derived from the use of Latin, also found in the short story "The Marriage of Mr. Anselme des Tilleuls," first translated in another volume in the Palik series, *The Marriage of a Marquis*.

An Adopted Son uses the theme of the suitor rejected for social reasons. Isidore, to marry the Baron's niece, hatches a scheme: to be adopted by the Baron for saving his life. Instead, Isidore falls into the traps he has prepared, and is saved by the Baron. Ultimately, the Baron admires both Isidore's persistence, and fears that some day he might land him in real danger. Lacking a son of his own, he adopts the lower-class Isidore, and will allow him to marry the niece, thereby carrying on the family name.

Another version of this idea was found forty years later in Verne's amusing novel, *Clovis Dardentor* (1896). Two cousins, eager to inherit, try to adopt the title character by saving his life, but with the

A letter from Verne to Victorien Sardou, asking for his comments
on *The Adoptive Son*—if it will not take up too much of his time.
Courtesy Volker Dehs Collection.

Transcription/translation on facing page.

Transcription

Jeudi soir,

Mon cher Sardou,

   Voici le fils adoptif qui ne réclame de vous qu'un quart d'heure d'attention. Cela vous va ou cela ne vous va pas. Si vous vous croyez obligé d'y consacrer une demi-journée de travail, c'est trop, et renonçons-y.

   Demain, je viendrai frapper à votre seconde porte, dite la porte des importuns, et réclamer votre bout de papier pour Déjazet. De cette façon, si vous voulez le préparer d'avance, vous ne serez aucunement dérangé.

   Enfin ! Pour 15 F. j'ai eu deux fauteuils pour ce soir ! – Et l'on ose médire des marchands de billets !

   Votre tout dévoué

Jules Verne

Translation

Thursday evening

My dear Sardou,

   Here is the Adopted Son who will take only a quarter of an hour of your attention. It will please you or it will not. If you feel obliged to work on it half a day, that would be too much, and we will abandon it.

   Tomorrow I will come knocking at your second door, called the door of the importuns, asking for your little paper for the Déjazet. So, in this way and if you could prepare it in advance, you won't be disturbed in any way.

   Finally, I managed, for 15 francs, to have two seats for this evening! And some people say nasty things about the ticket sellers!

   Your most devoted

Jules Verne

The letter can be dated from around 1860 because Verne is asking for an introduction paper for the theatre Déjazet where Sardou had his two *first* successes (*Les premières armes de Figaro* in 1859, and *Les Pattes de mouche*, a distant adaptation of Poe's "The Purloined Letter," in 1860). The date "1853" has been added on the manuscript long afterwards.

same outcome that Isidore experiences. However, when Dardentor's friend Louise saves him, he agrees to sanction her marriage to one of the cousins—who thus becomes a relative of Dardentor, if only by marriage.

The Adoptive Son is the second of four collaborations between Wallut and Verne. The others were the drama *La Tour de Montlhéry* (*The Tower of Montlhéry*, 1852), the comedy *Eleven Days of Siege*, the "opéra bouffe" *Les Sabines* (*The Sabines*, 1867), and *An American Nephew*. Wallut was a playwright, editor and French financier, born December 3, 1829 in Ville-sous-la-Ferte. He studied law in Paris, receiving his doctorate in 1854. In Brussels he married Mathilde Sachman (1835-1922) in 1855 and had four children.

In 1849, Wallut began working at the magazine, *Musée des Familles* (*Family Museum*); his father, Ferdinand, managed the company which financed the publication. The magazine was also important to Verne. By the time of this play he had published three stories there: "Un drame au Mexique--Les premiers navires de la marine mexicaine" ("A Drama in Mexico—The First Ships of the Mexican Navy") appeared in July 1851, "Un Drame dans les airs" in August 1851, and *Martin Paz* in July 1852. The latter two, a fantasy and an adventure, were almost immediately translated into English, his first such appearances. "A Voyage in a Balloon" was in the May 1852 issue of *Sartain's Union Magazine of Literature and Art* in the United States, and in England in the July 24, 1852 issue of *The Working Man's Friend and Family Instructor*. *Martin Paz* was retitled *The Pearl of Lima* in the April 1853 issue in volume 42 of *Graham's Magazine*, a Philadelphia monthly. Nonetheless, despite this measure of international success, the stories won Verne no particular notice.

Wallut would become editor of *Musée des Familles* from 1863 to 1881, publishing even more of his friend's stories, including *Les Forceurs de blocus* (*The Blockade Runners*, 1865), *Une fantaisie du Docteur Ox* (*A Fancy of Doctor Ox*, 1872), and *Le Comte de Chanteleine: Un Episode de la Revolution* (*The Count of Chanteleine: A Tale of the French Revolution*, 1864). The latter is translated for the first time in another volume of the Palik series.

In other ways, the *Musée des Familles* gave evidence of Verne's influence, publishing some new comedies, chronicles and literary and scientific studies, including novels similar to Verne's. One was

An 1858 newspaper caricature of the club Onze-sans-femmes
(Eleven Without Women). From top, unknown, Charles Wallut,
Aristide Hignard, Verne, unknown. Courtesy Volker Dehs Collection.

dedicated to Verne, while another, Wallut's novel *Sur le rives de l'Amazone—Voyage d'un femme: Marthe Verdier* (*On the banks of the Amazon—Travels of a woman: Marthe Verdier*, 1869), had resonances with Verne's *La Jangada* (*The Jangada*, 1881), *Mistress Branican* (1891), and *Le Superbe Orénoque* (*The Mighty Orinoco*, 1898). Wallut's family was part of the small colony of friends that liked to join Verne for cruises aboard his yacht, *Saint-Michel*. Using his pseudonym of Charles Raymond, Wallut published several articles including one about Verne, appearing in the September 1875 issue of *Musée des Familles*.

In 1869, Wallut launched a magazine called *Le Monde des enfants, nouveau journal de la jeunesse* (*The World of Children, a New Journal for Youth*), but it failed. Later Wallut financial endeavors had better results; he took part in the creation of the Crédit Foncier, the Immobilière Marseillaise (Marseillaise Estate) and the Société du Canal sous la Manche (Canal Company under the English Channel). He died on September 29, 1899 at Saint-Germain-en-Laye.

CHARACTERS

BARON d'ENTREMOUILLETTES, aged 50

CESARINE, his niece

DUMORTIER, his friend, aged 50

ISIDORE BARBILLON, Dumortier's nephew

IPHARAGHERRE, a Basque Guard

LAURENT, the Baron's house servant

The action takes place in Dumortier's park in Navarre. A pavilion to the right. At the back a wooden bridge thrown up over a small stream. Rustic chairs.

DUMORTIER: *(to Isidore)* And Miss Cesarine?

ISIDORE: I just met her taking her usual stroll through the park.

DUMORTIER: The fact is she's as early a riser as her uncle the Baron is a late one. Since my noble friend accepted hospitality in the pavilion in my park he's been rising so late that he's been obliged to lunch alone. We are in that case deprived of the honor—

ISIDORE: Why the honor?

DUMORTIER: You don't know that the d'Entremouillettes are the principal nobility of Sologne?

ISIDORE: Well? And so what?

DUMORTIER: So what! So what! As for you—heavens, you will never understand anything about these things.

ISIDORE: It's quite possible.

DUMORTIER: *(to Ipharagherre)* And you, Ipharagherre?

IPHARAGHERRE: I was telling you, Mr. Dumortier, that this reminds me of the story of Lampourdan and D'Etcheverry.

DUMORTIER: Ipharagherre, my friend, keep for another time your Basque stories and tell us what you've discovered?

ISIDORE: If he's found something—

IPHARAGHERRE: As to that, Mr. Dumortier, according to your instructions, after one day and two nights, it's not for us to boast, we beat a path, but with Basque legs, we would go to the end of the world headfirst.

ISIDORE: Uncle, the tales of this guard distress me. *(sitting down)*

DUMORTIER: *(to Ipharagherre)* For once in your life, can't you go straight to the point when you're telling something?

IPHARAGHERRE: Ah! Sir, it's difficult to go straight in mountainous country; it's easy for you to talk like that—If Etcheverry and Lampourdan were here—

ISIDORE: If they were here we'd have to go because the place would be untenable. Set three Basques to tell a story! The devil—

DUMORTIER: For the last time, Ipharagherre, will you tell me, yes or no, if my instructions were followed, if you discovered?

IPHARAGHERRE: Well, yes, Mr. Dumortier, we discovered! By dint of running through the mountain, by excavating the woods, by ferreting through the dens—we discovered a bear—

DUMORTIER: A bear!

IPHARAGHERRE: A magnificent bear! With tracks as long as this—I will show you when you like.

DUMORTIER: But—

IPHARAGHERRE: Oh! It's very close by; we even succeeded with Lampourdan.

ISIDORE: And Etcheverry—

IPHARAGHERRE: And Etcheverry is bringing the beast quite near you, and at this time, it's prowling in the environs. It already ate two calves and I swear to you that it wouldn't be wise to stroll there without being armed to the teeth.

DUMORTIER: Two calves! What a bruiser! Certainly I'd like a bear, a little bear.

ISIDORE: A fanciful, whimsical bear, a chimera. Ah, really, uncle, what the devil do you want to do with a bear! Are you going to become a hunter now?

DUMORTIER: Me! Hunter! Me mingle with dogs, grapple by trickery with a partridge, or outsmart a jack rabbit.

ISIDORE: Or the malice of a bear.

DUMORTIER: Like you say, a bear! Never; no, that's not me; that's for my worthy friend, the Baron Gulistan d'Entremouillettes.

ISIDORE: Ah! Ah! Ah! It's for the Baron!

DUMORTIER: In his high caste, the taste for the hunt is traditional; so I didn't want him to leave Navarre without having had the pleasure of killing a bear in the open mountains.

IPHARAGHERRE: And if he kills this one, he'll be killing a beauty, for, saving your respect, Mr. Dumortier, if it caught you, it wouldn't even make a mouthful of you.

DUMORTIER: Oh! A mouthful or two, if he gets me—the thing is not to be gotten.

ISIDORE: That's it.

IPHARAGHERRE: But you, Mr. Barbillon, you have the air of spitting on it.

ISIDORE: Me! Spit on a bear—If it was a bear rug, I don't say.

IPHARAGHERRE: Because it's a nasty beast, believe me, and despite all your science, your study of law, your rubrics of the code, it would know well enough how to put you down!

ISIDORE: Yes! Down in its stomach! I don't doubt it, that's why I will avoid making it my habitual companion. I don't know if the Baron will be very flattered—

DUMORTIER: I hope so, but my noble friend's really late putting in an appearance; could he have spent a bad night? It's my duty to inform myself.

(Dumortier rings at the pavilion door. Laurent enters.)

DUMORTIER: The Baron—?

LAURENT: *(razor in hand)* I have the honor of doing the Baron's beard. *(goes back in)*

ISIDORE: With the razor of his ancestors!

DUMORTIER: Fine! He won't delay emerging to take his chocolate in the fall air. You know that by a delicacy quite worthy of his race he has himself accompanied by his silverware when he's travelling, and never eats except with settings bearing his monogram. *(to Ipharagherre)* Therefore, Ipharagherre, prepare yourself, warn your friends.

ISIDORE: Etcheverry and Lampourdan! Take careful precautions so that no harm comes to this especially worthy—

IPHARAGHERRE: But at what time will the Baron d'Entremouillettes deign to set forth on the hunt?

DUMORTIER: You're right, we need to know. *(rings)* The Baron—

LAURENT: *(appearing, dressing gown in hand)* I have the honor of combing the Baron's wig— *(he goes back in)*

DUMORTIER: Well, my friend, I cannot allow myself to persist and to tear my noble friend from his grave occupation. Hold yourself ready, that's all that I can tell you.

IPHARAGHERRE: We'll be ready.

ISIDORE: And advise your bear, if sometimes he takes you in his confidence, not to make a nasty rush at the Baron who is to have the honor of killing him.

IPHARAGHERRE: Laugh! Laugh! Mr. Isidore, if you only knew the adventure that happened to Lampourdan and Etcheverry the night of—

ISIDORE: No! I don't wish to know it.

DUMORTIER: Go! Ipharagherre, go! Everything happens suitably.

(Ipharagherre leaves.)

ISIDORE: Since I find myself alone with you, uncle, I must confess a secret to you and request a service of you.

DUMORTIER: At your ease, my dear boy, I'm listening to you.

ISIDORE: The thing is, I don't know where to begin.

DUMORTIER: At the end!

ISIDORE: Well, in that case—! I love—

DUMORTIER: Hang on a sec! I am thinking—if the Baron's not a hunter— *(goes to the pavilion and rings)* The Baron—

LAURENT: *(appearing, horn in hand)* I have the honor of shoeing the Baron. *(goes back in)*

ISIDORE: With the horn of his fathers!

DUMORTIER: Have you noticed how respectful his servants are. No, I'm with you—You were saying before?

ISIDORE: I was saying before, uncle, beginning at the end—that I love Miss Cesarine.

DUMORTIER: *(stupefied)* Miss Cesarine?

ISIDORE: Miss Cesarine.

DUMORTIER: Miss Cesarine d'Entremouillettes?

ISIDORE: Herself!

DUMORTIER: What's this! She loves you?

ISIDORE: Excuse me! I didn't say she loves me; I said "herself" in person.

DUMORTIER: The niece and ward of Baron Gulistan d'Entremouillettes?

ISIDORE: His own niece and ward.

DUMORTIER: You! Isidore Barbillon?

ISIDORE: My very self.

DUMORTIER: Son of Jean Barbillon and Claudine Tournecerf.

ISIDORE: As you say—

DUMORTIER: A lawyer with no cases?

ISIDORE: With no cases, but not without effect.

DUMORTIER: But have you considered, wretch, the distance which separates you? And first off, Miss Cesarine is the sole heir of her uncle, two or three times a millionaire, while from my succession, your only fortune is small enough, but that's not all.

ISIDORE: I know it.

DUMORTIER: Were you ten times richer and a hundred times more celebrated the Baron would never consent to such a mesalliance. Think of it! A Barbillon.

ISIDORE: All this is true, uncle, and I said it to myself. But what do you want? I love Miss Cesarine.

DUMORTIER: And how did this catastrophe occur?

ISIDORE: In a quite simple way. How does love happen! Does anyone know? Here it is a month that the Baron's been installed in this park with his charming niece! Here it is a month that I met her strolling, book in hand, picking flowers by nature less fresh and charming than she. We talked, we laughed: I offered her my hand to cross over a stream, she leaned on my arm so as not to wet her charming little feet; I pulled back the branches which could hurt her sweet face, and I got myself scratched in her place; which proves I am ready to shed all my blood for her! So goes love, uncle, we first met by chance, now we meet on purpose, without the time of the rendez-vous having been agreed between us. Miss Cesarine clings little, I think, to her noble lineage; her mother was as plebian as you and I, something the Baron never forgave in his brother. In short, what can I tell you? I began my story at the end, and I will even end it there. Miss Cesarine is twenty, I'm twenty-five; we are alone, find a better reason for a brave lad to love a pretty girl, and that's why I love Miss Cesarine!

DUMORTIER: The fact is that it's very original! But you are going to ruin me in the mind of my noble friend: he will think I am embroiled in aiding this conspiracy. He will never consent to kill a bear that I am offering him under conditions like this!

ISIDORE: I am counting on you, my dear uncle, to make my demand!

DUMORTIER: That's all that was lacking! Don't think of it, wretch, don't think of it. But, at least, Miss Cesarine loves you?

CESARINE: *(entering)* What is it that one calls love, Mr. Dumortier?

DUMORTIER: Ah! Miss!

ISIDORE: Miss Cesarine!

DUMORTIER: What is it one calls love? My word, I don't know. To tell the truth, the nature of my preoccupations not having permitted me to fathom it—delve into it—I don't know.

CESARINE: Well, Mr. Dumortier, if a man, reflective, intelligent, and wise like you, doesn't know the word to love, how do you expect that a poor young girl can ever know it?

DUMORTIER: Miss, the word to love is a verb.

ISIDORE: A verb of the first conjugation, the first that one learns to conjugate in all languages, phidero in Greek, amo in Latin, I love in French. It's an active verb that governs a direct object. When we get out of college, if we want to profit from the Humanities, we have nothing more to do in this world than to seek out this charming direct object, to attach ourselves to it with eternal fetters. Uncle, I've met this direct object, here it is, it's Miss Cesarine and in seeing her so beautiful, so sweet, so perfect, no one will dare say I didn't do well at my studies.

CESARINE: Oh! Mr. Isidore, you make me confused! Happily, your uncle is here to reply to you and to tell you how much you exaggerate.

DUMORTIER: I didn't say that. Only my nephew is completely unworthy of you, under all accounts, of you and of your uncle and tutor, Baron D'Entremouillettes.

CESARINE: My uncle loves me, Mr. Dumortier, and when he sees that it is my dearest wish, perhaps he will sacrifice his haughtiness to my happiness.

DUMORTIER: I don't wish to make you despair Miss, but—

ISIDORE: If the Baron refuses, we will see what has to be done! Or if necessary to begin with that, made to refuse immediately.

DUMORTIER: What, you are going abruptly—without preparation?

ISIDORE: Abruptly! From what I can see the opportunity is favorable.

CESARINE: Courage, Mr. Isidore.

DUMORTIER: Wait, at least until he's killed my bear!

ISIDORE: Thanks, I will die a bachelor waiting for that.

DUMORTIER: The door's opening. I'm getting out of here.

ISIDORE: No, stay there! I will speak publicly.

LAURENT: *(announcing from the doorway)* Monsieur Le Baron Gulistan d'Entremouillettes.

DUMORTIER: Ah! Milord Baron

BARON: What's this? My dear Dumortier, I think.

DUMORTIER: *(aside to Isidore)* He said: My dear Dumortier.

ISIDORE: *(aloud)* Sir—

BARON: Ah! Mr. Isidore, I imagine—

ISIDORE: *(aside)* He imagines all the time! What a man.

BARON: Ah! It's you, Cesarine.

CESARINE: Did you sleep well, uncle?

BARON: Slept nobly, Cesarine. And you?

CESARINE: Just fine, uncle.

BARON: I love to think that your dreams have been worthy of your birth, and that our family has nothing to blush for.

CESARINE: Nothing! *(low to Isidore)* I was thinking of you, Mr. Isidore.

ISIDORE: Dear Cesarine.

LAURENT: Will the Baron honor these trees by lunching in their shade?

BARON: Yes! Laurent, have me served here. I feel myself in appetite this morning.

(Laurent sets up a small table on which he places settings that he takes from the pavilion.)

DUMORTIER: I am delighted that the air of our mountains is favorable to you, Baron.

BARON: Yes! It's nice enough air, and it agrees perfectly with the lungs of the rest of us; does it agree with you, too?

ISIDORE: Yes, indeed, Baron; it's not our fault if we breathe the same air as you, but—

BARON: Breathe, gentlemen, breathe, I allow you to!

ISIDORE: You are quite good, sir.

LAURENT: If the Baron will honor this table by his presence?

DUMORTIER: Does the Baron find these eggs cooked sufficiently?

BARON: Yes. These are eggs from the parish chicken?

DUMORTIER: Alas! I don't have thoroughbred chickens in my farm yard; may the Baron excuse me. But as for the eggs, I can attest to the Baron that they have been cared for in a special manner and laid according to his wishes.

BARON: Fine, Dumortier. At home, I'm accustomed to paint my coat of arms on the eggs I eat, but here—

DUMORTIER: I regret it—If I'd known—. . . If the Baron—

ISIDORE: *(to Dumortier)* Uncle, don't speak to him in the third person, you sound like his servant.

DUMORTIER: As for me—I— *(wants to serve the Baron something to drink)*

BARON: Excuse me, you know outside my home, I drink only water!

DUMORTIER: Still, it's from the Hermitage of 1834.

BARON: Let's see! Yes, not too bad.

ISIDORE: You must have curious arms on your coat of arms, Baron.

BARON: Certainly! Do you know something of the art of heraldry—Mr.— Isidore.

ISIDORE: We lawyers are actually forced to know a little bit of everything.

BARON: Well, we bear arms, the left hand an ermine banner, bearing these terrible words for a device: Save yourself if you can.

DUMORTIER: Marvellous! Splendid!

ISIDORE: *(aside)* Idiot! Brute!

LAURENT: If the Baron wishes to do these snipe the honor—

BARON: Willingly. Mr. Dumortier you will say on our behalf to your chef that the Baron d'Entremouillettes is satisfied with him.

DUMORTIER: He will be very much honored, Baron.

BARON: You've got nice enough hunting country here.

DUMORTIER: Excellent! Small game, big game, birds and animals.

BARON: Hunting is a noble amusement; it recalls the rough traditions of war; we used to be a great hunter.

DUMORTIER: Well, Baron, that encourages me to speak to you of an excursion I set up with the object of being pleasant for you.

BARON: Speak, Dumortier. I am listening to you.

DUMORTIER: It's a question of a bear hunt.

BARON: A bear hunt. Zounds, that suits me.

DUMORTIER: My huntsman has beat up one of these magnificent animals in the Baron's honor.

BARON: *(rising)* Fine, Dumortier. We will thank you for your efforts in rendering our stay agreeable! A bear! By Jove he'll be well received; it's truly a royal game, with which our great King Henry more than once battled in these mountains. A bear. Laurent, you are to go immediately to prepare my outfit for the hunt. Go, and don't keep me waiting.

(Laurent leaves.)

DUMORTIER: Baron, I'm enchanted that you are taking the matter to heart.

BARON: Will you accompany us?

DUMORTIER: I am not in a very bellicose mood, but perhaps, my nephew?

BARON: The gentleman will be welcome in our suite.

CESARINE: Uncle, you won't expose yourself.

BARON: Don't worry, niece, we know these sports, and we ourselves will bring you one of the monster's paws.

CESARINE: *(to Isidore)* He seems well disposed. Try.

DUMORTIER: *(to Isidore)* I beg you, nephew, don't say a thing! You're going to ruin my hunt.

CESARINE: Go on.

ISIDORE: It's not easy.

CESARINE: Courage, I'm here!

ISIDORE: Baron, I have a request to make you; but above all I beg you to excuse the boldness of it.

BARON: Speak, sir, we don't abhor bold things.

DUMORTIER: I don't have any idea where this will lead.

ISIDORE: Baron, I love Miss Cesarine, your niece, and I have the honor of requesting her hand.

BARON: Huh!

DUMORTIER: Believe, indeed—

BARON: Sir, above all I recognize the frankness of your request; you used the phrase exactly as it is customarily used in such circumstances.

ISIDORE: Baron!

BARON: Mr. Barbillon I will reply as uncles always reply to the aforesaid phrase: I am very honored by your request, but—

CESARINE: Uncle, dear uncle—

BARON: Cesarine, you will immediately go to your room, where you will await my supreme instructions. *(Cesarine leaves, making a sign of friendship to Isidore)* You, gentlemen, kindly listen to me.

DUMORTIER: But the bear that has the honor of awaiting the Baron—

BARON: He shall wait, sir, and I don't think he will be dishonored by waiting. Gentlemen, in the ninth century, one of my ancestors, Renaud d'Entremouillettes, was the Senechal of King Louis the Meek— that means supervisor of the Royal Mansion.

ISIDORE: *(aside)* My great-great grandfather was a servant in an honorable family, which is similar.

BARON: In the tenth century, Godefroy d'Entremouillettes was Constable to King Robert, meaning charged with his stables.

ISIDORE: *(aside)* My grandfather was a groom which is almost the same thing.

BARON: During the Crusade, the Lords d'Entremouillettes accompanied their king into the holy land, and were more or less killed there while bequeathing to their grandsons an imperishable glory and nobility. Do you insist on marrying a d'Entremouillettes, sir?

ISIDORE: I insist, Baron.

DUMORTIER: *(aside)* How's this going to turn out?

BARON: I haven't spoken to you of the actual and future fortune of Cesarine, my heir, because you know the case I make from money, but you will understand, without need to persist a long while, that a d'Entremouillettes cannot be called Madame Barbillon.

ISIDORE: Still—

BARON: I have the honor of telling you that nine d'Entremouillettes took part in nine crusades.

ISIDORE: Ah! Sir, there were thousands of Barbillons at the time of the flood.

BARON: We never had relations with any of them, sir. As to the rest, you don't displease me, Mr. Isidore, on the contrary, you're a very fine lad.

ISIDORE: *(modestly)* Oh! Oh!

BARON: I don't say that you have the great appearance of Anne d'Entremouillettes, my ancestor, but you are a fine lad, you have wit, but for God's sake, why have you such a disagreeable label. Just call yourself de Luynes or Montmorency and my niece is yours.

ISIDORE: You are really good. Would you like to read in the Monitor tomorrow: Mr. Isidore Barbillon requests to bear the name Montmorency under which he's never been known.

DUMORTIER: What a joke!

BARON: Dumortier, do you feel the need to know what would have been my life's dream?

DUMORTIER: I feel the need, Baron.

BARON: To have a son, bearing my name and to marry him to my niece! I am, as you know, the last offshoot of the great race of Entremouillettes, after me the name goes out like a lamp.

ISIDORE: Needing oil.

DUMORTIER: Why didn't you marry, Baron?

BARON: I married nine times.

ISIDORE: As many women as crusades, that was your way of crusading.

DUMORTIER: And you never had children?

BARON: Never! I beg you to believe it wasn't my fault.

DUMORTIER: Why, then, Baron, why haven't you adopted some young lad who would have borne you name and perpetuated your line?

BARON: Eh, Dumortier, was it to be supposed that a d'Entremouillettes would marry nine times without being able to obtain an offspring?

DUMORTIER: That was contrary to all supposition.

BARON: Besides, I had thought of it, but to adopt, it would have been necessary to give to a child during his minority the cares foreseen by the code, but I am not in the situation—

DUMORTIER: My! My! Why, I, who raised Isidore—if the name Dumortier agrees with you more than that of Barbillon.

BARON: One's as good as the other.

ISIDORE: You can also—

BARON: Nothing, sir, and my name will expire! *(rising)* I think I've made you sufficiently comprehend my intentions. I won't hide from you that Mr. Barbillon's request has painfully affected me and I prefer to believe, Dumortier, that you were not an accomplice in his boldness.

DUMORTIER: Milord Baron—

BARON: I must separate myself immediately with my niece, but above all, I want to kill this bear you offered me. I'll leave tonight because Miss Cesarine d'Entremouillettes must not stay any longer beneath this roof.

ISIDORE: Baron—

BARON: Sir, I have spoken.

(Enter Ipharagherre.)

IPHARAGHERRE: Mr. Dumortier, Milord Baron—

BARON: What's the matter? Speak my lad.

IPHARAGHERRE: Saving your respect, Etcheverry and Lampourdan just noticed the bear a quarter of an hour from here; if you want to, there's just time enough!

BARON: I am running to put on my hunting equipment. I will rejoin you my friend, take your best precautions and don't lose sight of the beast.

IPHARAGHERRE: I'll watch for you, Milord.

(Ipharagherre leaves and the Baron goes into the pavilion.)

DUMORTIER: Well, wretch, you didn't want to listen to me, not only have you been roughly thanked, but you are making me lose the company of the Baron.

ISIDORE: *(joyous)* Don't worry, uncle. I'm more determined than ever.

DUMORTIER: What do you mean?

ISIDORE: You spoke with the Baron of adoption, and he himself was already thinking of it; but do you know what the consequences of adoption are?

DUMORTIER: Almost.

ISIDORE: The adoptee becomes the true child of the adopter to the point that he is constituted *hic et nunc* his legitimate heir and he takes his name.

DUMORTIER: Well?

ISIDORE: Well, I will be delighted that Cesarine is not called Madame Barbillon, but the Baroness d'Entremouillettes.

DUMORTIER: I don't see how the Baron could adopt you, my poor Isidore, supposing he were to agree to it, since he did not render to you during your minority the required care.

ISIDORE: First of all, it's completely agreed, isn't it, that the Baron will be adopting no matter who in order that his name can be perpetuated to future ages?

DUMORTIER: It's one of the prejudices of his class, and I think if one furnished him the means—

ISIDORE: Well! I will furnish him the means.

DUMORTIER: You!

ISIDORE: You recall your legal training?

DUMORTIER: No! Perhaps it contains something I've never known about.

ISIDORE: Well, listen—article 345. "The capacity to adopt cannot be exercised except towards an individual to whom one has, in his minority and for at least six years furnished assistance and given uninterrupted care."

DUMORTIER: Well?

ISIDORE: Hold on! *(continuing)* "Or instead, someone who has saved the life of the adopter, be it in combat or by saving him from fire or drowning." Do you get it?

DUMORTIER: Great God! What do you intend to do?

ISIDORE: To sew perils beneath the feet of the Baron, and to save him from them despite him.

DUMORTIER: But the opportunity! He intends to leave tonight.

ISIDORE: The opportunity's been found.

DUMORTIER: Huh! What?

ISIDORE: The combat, the battle—do you think that if I snatch him from the claws of the bear, that won't count for combat?

DUMORTIER: Doubtless, but—

ISIDORE: That's my business.

CESARINE: *(entering)* Well?

ISIDORE: Victory, Miss, victory!

CESARINE: My uncle—

ISIDORE: Absolutely refused.

CESARINE: But in that case?

ISIDORE: I've got it! Be confident and prepare all your thanks for Ipharagherre's bear!

CESARINE: The bear!

IPHARAGHERRE: *(entering)* The bear—you can hear him roaring!

ISIDORE: Your uncle! Silence.

BARON: *(entering dressed in hunting costume)* Are we leaving?

IPHARAGHERRE: Let's be on our way, Milord Baron.

BARON: You are not going to accompany us, Dumortier?

ISIDORE: No, my uncle prefers to stay, but as for me, I will accompany you, Baron.

BARON: Let's leave then!

IPHARAGHERRE: The bear isn't a hundred feet from the park.

ISIDORE: On our way and good hunting.

BARON: Aren't you going to take a rifle?

ISIDORE: Go on! To kill a wretched bear! Besides, Baron, I will let you do it.

BARON: Zounds, on our way!

(Exit the Baron, Isidore and Ipharagherre.)

DUMORTIER: There's nothing to say, I must follow them.

CESARINE: But what's wrong with you, Mr. Dumortier, why, what's wrong with you? What's got into Isidore? What's he intend to do with that bear?

DUMORTIER: He's mad!

CESARINE: The bear is mad! Ah! My God!

DUMORTIER: No! My nephew! Not to mention he's perfectly capable of devouring your uncle.

CESARINE: Mr. Isidore? Devour my uncle?

DUMORTIER: No! The bear. And with his bold, adventurous, brave character he is capable of confronting him, hand to hand.

CESARINE: The bear?

DUMORTIER: No! Your uncle.

CESARINE: Explain yourself, I beg you, because I don't understand a thing, Mr. Dumortier, and I am asking myself who is crazy here.

DUMORTIER: Ah! Pardon me, Miss. How do you expect me to explain! All this is swirling in my brain! The bear, my nephew, your uncle! The first has unparalleled audacity, the other a mad plan, the third formidable claws. All this is mixing together, I no longer understand anything, and I am asking myself if your uncle isn't the bear's nephew or if the bear isn't the uncle of my nephew!

CESARINE: Mr. Dumortier, calm down! Mercy, put me au courant of the situation; you know I am brave, too; don't hide the truth from me—what happened between my uncle and Isidore?

DUMORTIER: Nothing! They reciprocated very pleasant words and then they brought up The Law: it appears that the Baron has not fulfilled the formalities. My nephew is very learned in the law: he passed all his exams with high grades, interesting research and a magnificent thesis on adoption.

CESARINE: But still they left together. Mr. Isidore seemed to be beside himself, could he have provoked my uncle?

DUMORTIER: Come on! He would throw himself in the fire for your uncle, I'll answer for that! Wait, Miss, if you must tremble I cannot hide it from you any longer—

CESARINE: Speak, speak!

DUMORTIER: Moreover, I don't wish to make myself accomplice to a crime!

CESARINE: To a crime!

DUMORTIER: Well, my nephew went—

CESARINE: Mercy—

DUMORTIER: To apply article 345 of the Code Napoleon—(*shouts and a rifle shot are heard in the distance*) What's that?

CESARINE: Shouting! Uproar!

DUMORTIER: It's coming this way.

CESARINE: The clamor's increasing.

DUMORTIER: Ah! The wretch!

CESARINE: What wretch?

DUMORTIER: My nephew! He must not have arrived in time.

CESARINE: In time!

DUMORTIER: And he must have let your uncle escape.

CESARINE: My uncle! Help!

(*Ipharagherre enters.*)

IPHARAGHERRE: Ah! What a misfortune! Such a brave man!

CESARINE: Why, speak!

IPHARAGHERRE: Miss

DUMORTIER: Well go on!

IPHARAGHERRE: Such a brave young man, Mr. Isidore.

CESARINE: Isidore wounded.

(*They bring Isidore in on a stretcher. The Baron follows him.*)

DUMORTIER: My nephew.

BARON: Place him there on that chair; it will be all right, a glass of water, quick.

(*Cesarine brings a glass of water.*)

DUMORTIER: But, what happened?

ISIDORE: *(coming to)* Where am I?

CESARINE: Isidore!

DUMORTIER: He's breathing! He's alive!

IPHARAGHERRE: Ah! Milord Baron, it's indeed to you that he owes still being of this world.

ISIDORE: What happened?

DUMORTIER: Isidore, the Baron is your savior.

ISIDORE: My savior! I'm ruined!

BARON: What's he say?

DUMORTIER: Nothing! Delirium!

ISIDORE: Fate! Got to start over!

CESARINE: But what happened?

BARON: Oh! Not much.

IPHARAGHERRE: Not much! Why the Baron is quite simply an admirable shot.

BARON: Oh! When one has been used to arms for thirteen centuries!

DUMORTIER: But still, explain yourself.

IPHARAGHERRE: It was like this. When the bear came to charge us, Lampourdan and Etcheverry were saying to me "Ipharagherre—"

ISIDORE: Enough, my friend, enough.

BARON: My God, nothing could be simpler; it must be thought that at the sight of our bear advancing on us, Mr. Isidore Barbillon lost his head, he rushed toward the beast. Your nephew rushed at him as if he had planned to attract it towards us. It was no use shouting at him Stop! Stop! Ipharagherre—

IPHARAGHERRE: And Lampourdan?

DUMORTIER: And Etcheverry?

BARON: Vainly wore out their lungs telling him: "Don't advance!" He kept going and throwing stones at the animal which sets off in pursuit of him. Mr. Isidore Barbillon turned back toward us but in his flight a root made him fall, then we shouted at him: "Don't budge! Play dead!"

DUMORTIER: Why, that's evident, it's very well known. When pursued by a bear the only thing to do is play dead.

ISIDORE: That was indeed my intention, uncle. I was stretched out there, holding my breath. The bear got there, sniffed me, turned me over, I didn't budge—when suddenly

CESARINE: My God!

ISIDORE: Judge the fatality. I fell with my nose in a tobacco plant and atchoo—I sneezed.

BARON: He sneezes! A dead man!

ISIDORE: The astonished bear first recoiled then came back at me. I lost my head and—

IPHARAGHERRE: And Milord Baron, who had come closer meanwhile, put a bullet in the heart of the animal which fell thunderstruck! Ah! What a shot.

ISIDORE: Baron, believe—

DUMORTIER: Believe, I beg you.

BARON: It was nothing! We thank you for your gratitude. But nothing is simpler. I see with pleasure that Mr. Barbillon is on his feet. I am enchanted to have done him this little service, and I am going to take leave of you, Dumortier.

DUMORTIER: But—

BARON: You know what I told you; Cesarine, prepare everything for your departure.

DUMORTIER: After all that's happened!

BARON: My decision is irrevocable.

ISIDORE: *(to Cesarine)* I have to speak to you, Miss.

BARON: I'm going back to my apartment while my valet is making the last preparations. Follow us, Cesarine.

LAURENT: *(opening the door to the pavilion)* The Baron Gulistan d'Entremouillettes.

DUMORTIER: I shan't leave him. *(he follows the Baron)*

ISIDORE: Miss Cesarine, I must tell you everything! What I did, it was for you, to force the Baron to adopt me, to give me his name, to share it with you!

CESARINE: That has really worked!

ISIDORE: It's worked very badly.

CESARINE: What, by getting yourself devoured by a bear you had the idea of obliging my uncle to give you my hand?

ISIDORE: It seems bizarre at first appearance: that's because I haven't explained to you—I wanted to rescue the Baron, but all is not lost.

CESARINE: My uncle's going to leave! He's taking me away.

ISIDORE: Oh! I've still got time.

ISIDORE: You've got time—to do what?

ISIDORE: Whatever happens, don't be frightened.

CESARINE: Still!

ISIDORE: If they tell you I'm a criminal, a murderer, don't believe it.

CESARINE: Huh?

ISIDORE: There's only one thing true in all this—it's that I love you.

BARON'S VOICE: Cesarine!

CESARINE: My uncle's calling me!

ISIDORE: Just another second!

CESARINE: Why, here! *(she gives him her hand)*

DUMORTIER: *(entering from the pavilion)* Impossible to keep him. What a devil of a man! Ah! Miss, the Baron is asking for you.

ISIDORE: One more word, that's all.

CESARINE: I can't, but here. *(gives him her hand again)*

ISIDORE: *(kissing it)* Thanks.

BARON'S VOICE: Cesarine!

CESARINE: I'm coming, I'm coming. *(goes into the pavilion)*

DUMORTIER: Ah, indeed, what do you intend to do?

ISIDORE: What I must, come what may.

DUMORTIER: And don't imagine that I am going to murder the Baron so you can come to his rescue!

ISIDORE: Uncle, do you love me?

DUMORTIER: Sure!

ISIDORE: And are you ready to second me, to assist in my marriage with Miss Cesarine?

DUMORTIER: Yes! In anything that is reasonable.

ISIDORE: Well, my plan is logical and I will follow it to the very end!

DUMORTIER: You are going to start attempting to draw the Baron into extraordinary perils again! Happily, I say happily now, he's leaving, and if he weren't leaving I would be ready to make him leave!

ISIDORE: Uncle, I failed the first time, I will succeed the second.

DUMORTIER: Ah, indeed! You're not going to start attracting bears—

ISIDORE: Don't worry! But I've sworn that Cesarine will be mine, and she will belong to me.

DUMORTIER: By Jove, don't get excited! You'll be doing stupid things again—What's your plan?

ISIDORE: Battle didn't succeed for me. We will see if water will be more favorable to me. Article 345—

DUMORTIER: What, you're going to drown the Baron?

ISIDORE: The law authorizes me to do it! On the condition that I save him.

DUMORTIER: Oh! These lawyers!

ISIDORE: It's necessary that I save him at all cost—or that he die! What's the depth of this river here?

DUMORTIER: Why, seven or eight feet at least.

ISIDORE: The devil!

DUMORTIER: And it runs very rapidly.

ISIDORE: Shoot! All the same, the die is cast!

DUMORTIER: Ah, indeed! Would you be planning to throw the Baron in the water?

ISIDORE: Don't worry: he will fall all alone, a board placed wrong, a false step, and there you go.

DUMORTIER: Why, wretch! That's quite simply a murder.

ISIDORE: Let it be whatever you like, but it's going to happen!

DUMORTIER: Ah! My dear nephew, in the end—

ISIDORE: Besides, if you oppose it, if you warn the Baron, I will blow my brains out.

DUMORTIER: There's not much to blow out. But sonofabitch! I will no longer live in the midst of crimes, rifle shots, ferocious beasts, drownings—

ISIDORE: For this to end, let me act. Besides, once the Baron's in the water, you understand plainly, that I am throwing myself after him.

DUMORTIER: But, do you know how to swim?

ISIDORE: Not the least bit.

DUMORTIER: Why, then—

ISIDORE: Then you will loan me your safety belt, with which you spent fine days at Biarritz during the last season.

DUMORTIER: He has an answer for everything!

ISIDORE: And I warn you of one thing: You don't have a minute to lose.

DUMORTIER: But my poor Isidore, my dear nephew, have you considered?

ISIDORE: I've considered too much! Will you, yes or no, get me that safety belt?

DUMORTIER: I will do it! What the devil! But explain to me how you count on using it. And be especially careful that the traps you are setting for the Baron don't fall on someone else—me for example.

ISIDORE: But get going! The belt or death! The Baron may leave from one moment to the next.

DUMORTIER: I'm going! I'm going.

ISIDORE: It's not a question of going. It's a question of running. But run! Run, will you!

(Dumortier leaves running.)

ISIDORE: *(alone) (If need be the scene on the bridge can take place in the wings)* And now to work! All I see here is a bit crazy, but only follies succeed. Let's see, the Baron to reach the park gate will necessarily proceed by this bridge. Now, what is this bridge? A simple plank resting on one shore of the river to the other. *(he moves it)* Well, that'll work by itself! If ever a bridge was destined to fold up under the feet of a passerby, this is really it. Fine. The balustrade is worm-eaten and won't withstand a shock. Couldn't do better! The step of a child would collapse this scaffolding—just like life—one sets foot on—the devil, the Baron.

(Baron enters with Laurent and Cesarine.)

LAURENT: To what carriage will the Baron confer the honor of transporting him?

BARON: The first coach we meet.

LAURENT: The Baron is not accustomed to travel in such dilapidated carriages.

BARON: It's necessary. I will wait in the next town for my horses to come get me.

ISIDORE: *(aside)* And my cursed uncle doesn't return!

CESARINE: Well, Mr. Isidore!

ISIDORE: Don't worry about a thing. *(aside)* I am in mortal anxiety.

LAURENT: At what time will the Baron have the honor of leaving?

BARON: Immediately, my bags are packed.

LAURENT: The trunks with the arms of the Baron d'Entremouillettes are completely locked. I will have them transported myself to the highway.

ISIDORE: And my uncle! My uncle!

BARON: *(to Laurent)* You will distribute this purse to the servants of Mr. Dumortier.

LAURENT: The Baron need not worry! I shall take care of the flunkeys.

(Laurent puts the purse in his pocket.)

BARON: And now, let's leave.

ISIDORE: My God!

BARON: *(heading towards the bridge)* Come—Cesarine.

ISIDORE: *(placing himself before the bridge)* Never!

BARON: Ah! Mr. Barbillon, I didn't see you. Are you well?

ISIDORE: Not bad! And you?

BARON: I am enchanted to meet you to pay you a last goodbye!

ISIDORE: Milord Baron, it is I, who after the service you rendered me —I couldn't let you leave without— *(aside)* And my uncle doesn't come.

BARON: Truce with gratitude; I only did what I must. You know the motto of our family: Save yourself if you can!

ISIDORE: *(aside)* Would it would please heaven that it were mine!

BARON: Come on, Cesarine.

ISIDORE: *(interposing)* A moment more. *(low to Cesarine)* Miss, prevent your uncle from going on the bridge!

CESARINE: Huh!

BARON: Well, Laurent, precede us!

ISIDORE: *(retaining him)* Laurent, my good, Laurent, mercy!

LAURENT: Sir, march before or behind the Baron, as your choose; it's an honor that I don't allow to just anyone.

ISIDORE: Laurent! Don't move!

BARON: Why, you are mad, sir!

ISIDORE: And my belt! My belt!

CESARINE: Why, uncle, shouldn't we wait for Mr. Dumortier to pay him our goodbyes?

BARON: Niece, if this house is well run, we will find the master of it at the gate of honor.

ISIDORE: No, indeed! He won't be there.

BARON: Well, so much the worse for him, sir. Let's be going, Laurent!

ISIDORE: *(beside himself)* No, Laurent. You shall not pass.

BARON: Well, we will see, Mr. Barbillon, if you will dare to oppose passage to Baron d'Entremouillettes.

(Laurent comes to Isidore.)

ISIDORE: Don't come any further! Don't come any further!

CESARINE: Uncle!

BARON: A d'Entremouillettes has never recoiled!

ISIDORE: *(struggling)* Help me!

(The Baron reaches the middle of the bridge and somersaults in.)

BARON: Ah!

LAURENT: Milord Baron!

ISIDORE: What did I tell you? Come what may.

(Hurls himself in the river.)

CESARINE: My uncle! Help! Run!

(Laurent leaves by the shore.)

DUMORTIER: *(Running in, belt in hand)* What's the matter?

CESARINE: My uncle! Isidore threw himself in after him.

DUMORTIER: He doesn't know how to swim.

CESARINE: Ah! *(she falls on a bench)*

DUMORTIER: The wretch! The wretches! They're struggling; they're fighting; the current's got them! Help!

(Enter Ipharagherre.)

IPHARAGHERRE: Ah! Two men in the water! Lampourdan, Etcheverry! Help!

DUMORTIER: *(looking)* Ah! They've reached the bank. They've caught a tree—they are saved! Ah! What a misfortune, what a shocking catastrophe.

IPHARAGHERRE: Here they are! Here they are!

(The Baron enters carrying Isidore in his arms.)

DUMORTIER: Saved! My God!

BARON: It's no reproach to him, but this is the second time I've saved this young man.

CESARINE: Ah! Uncle! He risked his life to save you.

DUMORTIER: Moreover, he doesn't know how to swim; but how did this happen?

BARON: Nothing could be simpler, as I was crossing over this bridge, behold one of the planks collapsed and I pitched head first into the river.

CESARINE: Ah! My God!

BARON: Relax! The misfortune wasn't great, I swim like a whale. But suddenly I felt myself seized by the collar; it was Mr. Barbillon.

DUMORTIER: Who was trying to pull you out of the water.

BARON: And who was pulling me to the bottom. I gave him a punch.

LAURENT: What an honor!

BARON: I stunned him and I pushed him in front of me toward the shore. There he is.

ISIDORE: Saved by him again. Always fate.

CESARINE: Mr. Isidore! I understand you! You intended—

ISIDORE: You see how it succeeded.

IPHARAGHERRE: Look, a glass of wine will set you up.

BARON: Laurent, bring back my trunks and come change me. *(goes into the pavilion)*

LAURENT: It's an honor for me, Milord. *(he follows him)*

DUMORTIER: As for you, Ipharagherre, follow me to prepare reviving cordials. *(he leaves)*

CESARINE: In the final reckoning, he still threw himself in the water to save my uncle. It's not his fault if the Baron knows how to swim. I'm going to fill my uncle in. *(she goes into the pavilion)*

ISIDORE: *(alone)* Fate's mixing in it. Ah! In the same day, I just missed being devoured by a bear and getting myself drowned! Well, still I will triumph! I am capable of everything, even great crimes! They will see what an unemployed lawyer is, and how he can eradicate an article of the Code when he has nothing to do! Brr! I'm soaked to the bone. I wasn't able to save this Baron from battle, nor from the waves, well, I will save him from the flames; this will warm me up in any case! To work. *(pulling matches from his pockets)* Fine! One won't light! *(trying another)* Two! It's always like this! Three! Nothing! Four! Nothing! Ah! How stupid I am. They are wet.

BARON: *(entering and striking him on the shoulder)* Enough, Mr. Isidore! You have so much luck today that I am still capable of saving you from flames.

ISIDORE: Huh?

DUMORTIER: *(entering)* What! What did he do?

ISIDORE: Damn! The third and last application of Article 345, uncle.

BARON: Hush.

ISIDORE: What's the matter?

(Isidore continues to strike the matches.)

BARON: *(to Dumortier)* Sir, I have the honor of presenting to you my adoptive son.

DUMORTIER: What are you saying?

ISIDORE AND CESARINE: Ah! Bah!

BARON: And the husband of my niece. It's the second time this young man saved my life.

IPHARAGHERRE: What about the bear?

BARON: He was the one who killed it.

ISIDORE: You think—Brr! I'm freezing.

DUMORTIER: What about the river?

BARON: He's the one who saved me.

ISIDORE: Again!

BARON: Weren't you present when he brought me back fainting in his arms?

CESARINE: Why, uncle, explain to me!

BARON: *(low)* Don't you understand this character will end by playing me a nasty trick, and since I have the opportunity to adopt him! *(aloud)* Mr. Isidore d'Entremouillettes, embrace your wife.

ISIDORE: Oh! Papa! *(to Dumortier)* Well! What do you say about the Civil Code?

DUMORTIER: I'm an uncle of a d'Entremouillettes. But, still, it really would have seemed to me—

BARON: What?

LAURENT: If the Baron does us the honor of telling us something—

IPHARAGHERRE: It's as if Lampourdan and Etcheverry were gone.

ISIDORE: Dear Cesarine!

BARON: My name will not perish! *(to Isidore)* Boys, have as many boys as possible!

ISIDORE: I have a secret. We never make anything else in my family.

Curtain

ELEVEN DAYS OF SIEGE

Victorien Sardou, Courtesy Volker Dehs Collection.

*O*nze jours de siege (*Eleven Days of Siege*) is a three-act comedy written by Verne with Charles Wallut and Victorien Sardou between 1857 and 1860. During Verne's lifetime, it was performed 21 times in 1861 (opening June 1 at the Théâtre du Vaudeville [Vaudeville Theatre]), three times in Amiens in 1880, and twice more there in 1900. *Onze jours de siege* was published as a 79 page booklet in Paris by Michel Lévy frères in 1861.

Wallut has been discussed in the preface to *The Adoptive Son*. Victorien Sardou was born September 5, 1831, in Paris and died there November 8, 1908. Along with Émile Augier and Alexandre Dumas *fils*, Sardou dominated the French stage in the late 19th century. He was elected to the Académie Française in 1877, a recognition Verne never received. Sardou, having written some 70 works, is still remembered as a craftsman of bourgeois drama, relying on theatrical devices to create an illusion of life. His popularity declined in the 20th century, although his last success, *Madame Sans-Gêne* (1893), is still performed.

In *Eleven Days of Siege*, a newlywed couple settle in Paris. The husband does not hesitate to abandon his young wife at home to keep up with past friends, and she quickly becomes jealous of his time away from her. Then a friend discovers the marriage itself may be invalid because a question arises as to the husband's French naturalization, since his father was a native of England. Which will prevail, love or marital disillusionment?

There are autobiographical reflections in the play. The name of the wife in *Eleven Days of Siege*, Laurence (the English form is Laura) recalls that in 1853, during a visit home to Nantes, Verne had fallen in love with a woman named Laurence Janmar. At a fancy-dress party, when she had complained to a female friend about the tight whalebone corset of her gypsy costume, Verne replied with a pun that may have been witty repartee in Paris but was too daring for the provinces. In fact, Janmar had been encouraging another suitor, whom she married a year later, leaving Jules distraught.

At the time he finished *Eleven Days of Siege*, Verne had, like the couple in the play, been married for three years, to Honorine de Viane Morel, a widow two years his junior with two young daughters. The situations described in the play and those in his life seem more than coincidental. Verne had already taken a trip to Scotland with Aristide Hignard, and in 1861 a Scandinavian trip with Hignard and Émile Lorois would return him home five days after the birth of Jules's son, Michel.

Eleven Days of Siege is a summation of Verne's romantic comedies for the theater, one of the final plays of his youth. In addition to his earlier published output in the adventure and fantasy genres for *Musée des Familles* (*Family Museum*) by the time of *Mr. Chimpanzee*, he had written numerous works in other genres, all of which remained unpublished during his lifetime. The novels *Un Prêtre en 1839* (*A Priest in 1839*, 1846), authored while still in his teens, featured a devil-worshipping cleric, and *Voyage à reculons en Angleterre et en Ecosse* (*Journey to England and Scotland*, 1859) fictionalized the trip with Hignard. "Pierre-Jean" told of a prisoner's escape, and was rewritten by Jules's son Michel for posthumous publication in 1910 as "La Destinée de Jean Morénas" ("The Fate of Jean Morénas"). "San Carlos" chronicled a Spanish brigand, and *Le Siège de Rome* (*The Siege of Rome*) was a historical chronicle; all four are to be translated for the first time in the Palik series, and another of the volumes, *The Marriage of a Marquis*, included the humorous "Le Mariage de M. Anselme des Tilleuls" ("The Marriage of Mr. Anselme des Tilleuls"). Verne had even written a serial of art criticism, providing a review of the Paris Salon of 1857, and drafted his first science fiction, *Paris au XXe siècle* (*Paris in the 20th Century*) in 1860. Though his record of actual publications was not imposing, this breadth of experience was about to allow the youthful playwright to turn into the best-selling novelist of the "Voyages Extraordinaires" ("Extraordinary Journeys").

CHARACTERS

ROQUEFEUILLE, notary

ROBERT MAUBRAY, age thirty

MAXIME DUVERNET, his friend

BAPTISTE, servant

LAURENCE, wife of Maubray, age twenty–two

LEONIE DE VANVRES, her friend, age twenty–four

THERESE, chamber maid

The action takes place in Paris in the 1860s.

ACT I

A room in Robert's home; doors to the right and left at the back; in the middle a chimney, a grandfather clock, vases of flowers, lighted candles; to the left a door, a round table; mid-stage a table, a bell, armchairs on each side, to the spectator's right, a door, a sofa.

AT RISE, Baptiste comes through the door at the left, then listens at the door.

BAPTISTE: You can hear them from here. *(coming forward)* My word! It's my opinion that when the masters are fighting at dinner, the servants are wise to get out. *(Ringing. Shrugging his shoulders he sits on the sofa)* It's true that complicates the service; you don't know if they are speaking seriously or joking. *(More ringing)* and you don't know what expression to wear, if you should smile or take on a grave manner.

ROBERT: *(entering)* Ah! So this is the way you come when you are called?

BAPTISTE: Sir, it's that—

ROBERT: That'll do—Bring me my overcoat and my hat.

(Laurence enters, dismisses Baptiste with a gesture; he bows slightly and leaves.)

LAURENCE: So, Robert, you've really decided to give yourself over this evening to bachelors? *(coming towards the right)*

ROBERT: Again! Ah, indeed, we're going to start all over again! Isn't it a matter that's agreed to?

LAURENCE: On the contrary, I was hoping that my remarks—

ROBERT: But your remarks are childish my dear friend; I don't intend, by taking them seriously, to makes us as ridiculous as they are!

LAURENCE: Ridiculous! Because you would have made a small sacrifice for me?

ROBERT: Eh! My God! Ask me something reasonable! But, I remind you, look!—To prevent me from going out this evening, going to this meeting—such a fantasy! A whim so puerile!

LAURENCE: I've seen time when you wouldn't even have dreamed of arguing.

ROBERT: Ah! That was really my fault, by God! It's from having, from the beginning, such an abnegation of my authority, that from concession to concession, you enjoy tyranny and my humiliation.

LAURENCE: Oh!

ROBERT: *(dwelling on it)* Yes! Humiliation! Truly, if I let you do it, I won't be a man, but a child led by the apron strings. I can neither leave nor return without consulting your good pleasure! And I would never go to see good friends at night, except stealthily, and by sliding along the wall like a man about to commit a crime.

LAURENCE: Oh! It's not a crime!

ROBERT: You're too good!

LAURENCE: But it's a fault!

ROBERT: Well, my darling Laurence, the wise sin seven times a day; so, I am within the limits of wisdom, because since this morning I've as yet committed only two faults!

LAURENCE: You are so modest! Which ones?

ROBERT: The first is to have spoken to you of this announced party, instead of dreaming up some pretext; the second is having debated with you my right to go there! I will therefore permit myself to commit a third, which will be to deliver myself to this soiree when the hour comes.

LAURENCE: You are making me understand a bit cruelly that you are the absolute master of your actions.

ROBERT: Look, Laurence, it's not serious is it? And this nasty quarrel is too harsh. Give me your little hand, and let's not speak of it anymore! I'm excitable and I get carried away— I'm wrong,—but be reasonable also, and don't sulk at me like a child! You have enough confidence in me so that ideas of independence shouldn't bear umbrage to you; I grant you the same rights, because I have the same confidence. And with all, the result is, in thinking it over carefully, we've been crazy right now and rather clumsy towards each other. (*going to embrace her*)

LAURENCE: (*rising*) Speak for yourself.

ROBERT: (*a bit annoyed*) So be it! As you like! Baptiste! (*Baptiste enters with coat and hat and leaves*)

LAURENCE: I thought this little debauch wasn't beginning until nine o'clock, and it's hardly—

ROBERT: It's the hour at which husbands decamp when wives want to cage them up.

LAURENCE: Very witty!

ROBERT: The spirit of Freedom, that's all! I would have had pleasure in keeping you company still, if you'd wanted to be more amiable; but I prefer to leave you than to continue the conversation in this tone; I'm leaving then; I'm going to my club, because my friend Maxime Duvernet gave me a rendez-vous there, because I must present him to my other friend, Horace. I don't know when I'll be back, because I don't know at what time this Roman orgy will end, and now my dear Laurence, after having responded to my inquisitor, my "because" has the honor of bowing to your "why"! *(he leaves by the back.)*

LAURENCE: No—he's distancing himself— *(listening)* He's gone! It's the first time that he didn't return to kiss me and to ask my pardon. Perhaps I was too severe, too? If I were to call him? He's too far away. And then, in the end, he's the one who's wrong, not me! To leave me alone! A whole evening! Oh! If he'd told me this that it would only take a year! And yet I ought to have suspected that the third year of marriage would be difficult to get through, the other two were so sweet—it couldn't last! *(hearing the door open)* What's that? I'm not at home to anybody!

ROQUEFEUILLE: *(entering)* Not even to your old friend Roquefeuille?

LAURENCE: Ah! Except for him! *(she offers him her hand)*

ROQUEFEUILLE: Thanks for the favor! But allow the elect to protest for the damned: a pretty girl has no right to flee the world like this and to deprive herself of the admiration of all. Here's for me! *(he extends his hand to her)* And here's for the others. *(he kisses her other hand several times)*

LAURENCE: *(withdrawing her hand)* Well, well, again!

ROQUEFEUILLE: *(continuing)* Hell! There's a crowd of 'em!

LAURENCE: You are gallant this evening, my dear notary!

ROQUEFEUILLE: Ah! Now there's a word which has the effect of ice on me! Don't call me notary if you appreciate my gallantry some little bit. Do I resemble a notary? Maxime ought to be here, where is he?

LAURENCE: He's not here.

ROQUEFEUILLE: And Robert?

LAURENCE: He's isn't here anymore.

ROQUEFEUILLE: Oh! Oh! The way you say that!

LAURENCE: Ah! My dear Roquefeuille, try to distract me, and be gay for the two of us, for I am very sad.

ROQUEFEUILLE: Is it possible? Tell me about this right away! What's the matter with you?

LAURENCE: Nothing—not even—my husband!

ROQUEFEUILLE: Robert the devil?

LAURENCE: Now there you are joking!

ROQUEFEUILLE: Ah! Ah! The situation's serious. You are saying to me: Be gay, without informing yourself if it's my time for it! I am making every effort, and you are not satisfied. There is something—

LAURENCE: Yes.

ROQUEFEUILLE: Well, are you going to confess? I know more than one ear that would be eager to hear the pretty sins of a woman! I am loaning you mine. Admit that your husband left as the result of a little discussion.

LAURENCE: Yes.

ROQUEFEUILLE: I suspected as much. And this discussion just came because you've never really understood the respective roles of spouses. Wait, look at the first carriage passing by. There's a man in the seat and a horse in the harness.

LAURENCE: That's their place!

ROQUEFEUILLE: Agreed! But why? The horse is stronger, and if it wanted to, it could carry away the man and the carriage, and it's he who leads it. So the man who knows it, bewares of irritating the horse, he flatters it, he caresses it with his voice, with his hand, and thanks to this mutual agreement, the carriage runs without accident. Well, dear lady, you leaned on the bridle too much and your husband is kicking.

LAURENCE: I fear it!

ROQUEFEUILLE: I was sure of it! Robert didn't leave—he escaped—he has the bit in his teeth.

LAURENCE: You think so?

ROQUEFEUILLE: It's evident! Ah! How right a great moralist was to say: Marriage is a battle to the end, before which spouses ask heaven for its blessing!

LAURENCE: Thanks, my dear notary!

ROQUEFEUILLE: Again! No more notary or I won't laugh anymore! And don't remind me of a profession that horrifies me!

LAURENCE: That horrifies you!

ROQUEFEUILLE: That horrifies me! A notary is serious, bureaucratic, earnest, zealous, one who inscribes, who makes contracts and who heaps frightful dossiers in boxes in his horrifying study, he's a public calamity! I denounce him to the hatred of his fellow citizens, to whom he loans his ministry to all the disasters of life. Mortgages, testaments, and marriages! The good, the true, the perfect notary, that's me! I don't take myself seriously, not me! Never! When a client consults me about the acquisition of real estate, I prove to him by A plus B that the land is in a mediocre location, or he'll reap less wheat than the law suit, and the client takes away his money. Let another one call me to receive his will and I demonstrate to him he's getting ready to make ingrates, and he decides to cure them. All profit! Finally, a third asks me to draw up a marriage contract, I escort him to the solicitor, my neighbor, whose specialty is separations, and from there to the Cafe Anglais, where I demonstrate the joys of bachelorhood through the fumes of champagne! And he gets married all the same—But in the end, he gets married!

LAURENCE: You must have a pretty clientele.

ROQUEFEUILLE: The most pretty clientele in Paris. An honest man always makes his way.

LAURENCE: You will end by converting me—and if my contract was to do over—

ROQUEFEUILLE: You would hurl the pen in the fire?

LAURENCE: I would sign it with both hands! I love my poor Robert so much!

ROQUEFEUILLE: He loves you, too, by God!

LAURENCE: No question, but not like he used to.

ROQUEFEUILLE: He's right to seek variety. Boredom is born the same day as uniformity.

LAURENCE: It's a long way from Paris to Mauritius, where we met each other, where we loved each other!

ROQUEFEUILLE: Three thousand leagues if you consult the Atlas.

LAURENCE: An immensity, if I consult his heart!

ROQUEFEUILLE: That's the rule! You are telling me about Mauritius. Consider Paul and Virginie, if Paul had married Virginie, where would Virginie be tonight? Beside the fireplace—and Paul at his club!

LAURENCE: Still, if it were just his club. But after the club, Paul and his friend Maxine must finish their evening with a bachelor reunion.

ROQUEFEUILLE: Well, so much the better.

LAURENCE: So much the better for whom?

ROQUEFEUILLE: For you. Your husband's reverting to bachelorhood, and you, you are reverting to being a young miss. On his return their will be a new marriage, that the two of you will contract.

LAURENCE: My dear Roquefeuille, I don't like to remarry so often.

ROQUEFEUILLE: It's still the best thing to do if you've been clumsy enough to marry the first time.

LAURENCE: *(laughing)* Heavens! You are impossible!

ROQUEFEUILLE: There you go! There's a smile!

LAURENCE: Ah! If you could only give me a way of preventing Robert from going to that party!

ROQUEFEUILLE: Get a warrant for his arrest.

LAURENCE: I would like something less violent.

ROQUEFEUILLE: Let's see if we can find one!

(Enter Baptiste.)

BAPTISTE: Madam—I beg madame's pardon—does madame know if monsieur will return soon?

LAURENCE: I am unaware—Why this question?

BAPTISTE: It's that—there's a very urgent letter for him.

LAURENCE: Well?

BAPTISTE: They brought it this morning; but I don't know how it happened.

ROQUEFEUILLE: You forgot it in your pocket?

BAPTISTE: Yes, sir.

ROQUEFEUILLE: What a breed!—All the same!

LAURENCE: Give me that letter. *(Baptiste leaves—to Roquefeuille)* This rush to leave—If it was a rendez-vous? A letter—

ROQUEFEUILLE: Come on, calm down, calm down, calm down—

LAURENCE: I don't have the strength. Here, look for yourself.

ROQUEFEUILLE: *(taking the letter and opening it)* A letter!

LAURENCE: *(excitedly)* A letter?

ROQUEFEUILLE: Of warning!

LAURENCE: *(joyfully)* Of warning?

ROQUEFEUILLE: And for tonight, even—It's not a drum, it's Fortune, in the guise of a police officer that brought this letter.

LAURENCE: What do you mean?

ROQUEFEUILLE: Allow me to give orders in your name. *(Calling)* Baptiste! *(Baptiste appears)* You are going to take this letter to your master at his club and you will deliver it to his own hands.

BAPTISTE: He is going to receive me very ill.

ROQUEFEUILLE: Ah! That's your affair, isn't it?

LAURENCE: Go! *(Baptiste takes a few steps.)*

BAPTISTE: *(returning)* Ah! Doctor Duvernet is asking if Mr. Roquefeuille is here.

LAURENCE: Maxine? Show him in!

(Baptiste leaves.)

LAURENCE: Now, my friend, what is your plan?

ROQUEFEUILLE: You haven't understood: your husband is in a relapsed state; it's prison for him. He cannot fail to obey, and my word, if he doesn't spend the night with his wife, he won't be spending it at his club, nor in the company of bachelors.

LAURENCE: Ah! It's true!—Is he going to be in a bad mood! Well, so much the better, let him be enraged.

(Laurence leaves by the right.)

ROQUEFEUILLE: Now there's a nasty wife, for goodness sake! And they want me to get married? Oh, no!

MAXIME: *(entering)* I just came from your place.

ROQUEFEUILLE: I was counting on finding you here.

MAXIME: I was hastening to announce my happiness to you! She's come, my friend.

ROQUEFEUILLE: She's come! Ah, bah! Who's she?

MAXIME: Why Leonie! The friend of Madame Maubray!

ROQUEFEUILLE: Madame de Vanvres! She! Leonie! A pronoun! A baptismal name! Why what sort of manners are these?

MAXIME: Eh! What better word than that of She! It says everything! It sums it all up! She! That means beauty, grace, wit—beloved, adored, venerated wife. She, the sole, the unique, the ideal—perfection itself! She! She, at last!

ROQUEFEUILLE: And him—brains blown out!—him—evaporated, him, senseless, the deranged, the mad, him at last!

MAXIME: Yes, yes, make fun of me! I am happy and I permit you to do it. I am young, I am rich, I'm neither hunchbacked, nor bandy-legged, nor twisted. I am a doctor, esteemed, loved, and I have only one passion in the world: traveling! It seems to forbid me love and especially marriage; how to hope that a woman would want to join her fate to that of a being so restless, so inconstant, so nomadic? Well, no! Fortune or rather heaven made me meet in Madame de Vanvres, a widow more passionate than myself for continual displacements, a frantic, irrepressible traveler! And, my friend, I hope to obtain the hand of this woman, to possess her and to take a world tour with her!

ROQUEFEUILLE: It's bewitching!

MAXIME: She's coming! I can publish the banns, prepare the contract, buy gloves and order the wedding presents.

ROQUEFEUILLE: And how do you know?

MAXIME: Ah! From a letter written to Madame Maubray which I got this morning—and here it is!

ROQUEFEUILLE: Covered with stamps of every color and all shapes, dirty, yellow with the dust of every chancellery! In your place I would put vinegar on it; I'd only hold it with pincers!

MAXIME: Cold and vulgar soul, read, read!

ROQUEFEUILLE: It's dated?

MAXIME: Last month. She's wandered on her way coming through Seville.

ROQUEFEUILLE: Ah, bah! Seville! I thought it existed only in novels. *(singing)* Do you know in Barcelona? *(resuming)* No! And this letter?

MAXIME: Ah! Only two lines, but two lines that, without mentioning my name, still reveal the most tender passion, the most true love.

ROQUEFEUILLE: Let's have a look at it. *(reading)* After leaving Seville, I am returning immediately to Paris by way of Naples and Switzerland.

MAXIME: Ah!

ROQUEFEUILLE: Ah, that's the most tender passion, the most true love! An itinerary!

MAXIME: What! You don't find this adorable? Returning to Paris—she—for me! And returning directly, even!

ROQUEFEUILLE: With quite a little detour—

MAXIME: To get here more quickly! To get here more quickly!

ROQUEFEUILLE: Ah! The two of you will make two pretty wackos.

MAXIME: Not at all, two comets, quite simply two comets, as for me that of 1828, she, that of 1832. We are describing immense angles through the whole world, but sometimes our orbits cross, and—

ROQUEFEUILLE: Ah! Really, no, no! You are becoming too flighty.

(Enter Robert.)

ROBERT: It's the work of misfortune! Don't they understand what's happening to me?—Hello, Maxime! At the moment in which I'm going to leave—Hello, Roquefeuille

MAXIME: What's wrong with you?

ROQUEFEUILLE: *(aside)* I've got a shrewd idea—

ROBERT: What's wrong with me? I just got a letter at my club!

MAXIME: A billet doux?

ROQUEFEUILLE: A bill to pay?

ROBERT: A letter of notice!

ROQUEFEUILLE: Ah, the devil!

ROBERT: And the worst is I've exhausted all warnings prior to discipline! Now it's impossible to go to that soiree!

ROQUEFEUILLE: *(aside)* Come on now!

MAXIME: Oh! As for me, I renounce it very willingly!

ROBERT: It's not that I cling to it unreasonably; for the prospect of a night spent side by side with my tailor and my bookmaker truly wasn't amusing.

ROQUEFEUILLE: All the same a camp bed is uncomfortable!

ROBERT: The devil take them! I won't go!

ROQUEFEUILLE: And prison?

ROBERT: That's right, prison! Ah, if I'd kept it, this drum!

ROQUEFEUILLE: You would beat the drum?

ROBERT: And, what's still more irritating, for this cursed soiree to which I cannot go any more, I almost quarrelled with my wife!

MAXIME: What! You've already had discussions about it with Madame Maubray?

ROQUEFEUILLE: If it's already gone that far, by Jove! Where do you expect to find yourself? You are married, that's what it is!

Big kids who won't jump in the water without knowing how to swim, and who hurl themselves head first into the abyss of marriage! You study ten years to be an engineer of bridges and highways, doctor or pianist, and you expect to divine, without learning it, this quite difficult art of being happy in living together—! Happy living together!

MAXIME: Always the same song!

ROQUEFEUILLE: Why, ignoramuses! Obstinate donkeys that you are—do you know that a German physiologist has published a work just on conjugal duties and that it runs to twelve volumes?

MAXIME: A real dictionary!

ROQUEFEUILLE: Yes, a dictionary from "a" amour! To "z" zero! All of marriage is there!

ROBERT: Look, I'm married, isn't that true? It's not the condition of marriage that worries me tonight, it's the condition of being a citizen.

MAXIME: Hold on, I am considering!

ROBERT: What?

MAXIME: Ah, indeed! So you are in the National Guard, are you?

ROBERT: That's what you call a consideration?

MAXIME: You've been naturalized as French since your marriage?

ROBERT: What's the good? What are you getting at?

MAXIME: At this: The French alone are admitted to the honor of serving in this institution: if Robert is not French; he can't be in the National Guard.

ROBERT: You would really please me by proving that paradox, for goodness sake; I was brought up in Mauritius, that's true, but I was born in the Faubourg Saint Germaine; my mother and father were French.

ROQUEFEUILLE: Indeed! The case seems settled to me. You are French, my dear fellow, go stand guard!

MAXIME: One moment!

ROQUEFEUILLE: Aesclapius demands the floor.

MAXIME: What Robert said is perfectly correct; but what he didn't say is that born in Paris, Faubourg Saint Germain, if his mother was French, he had a perfectly English father, a pure blooded Englishman.

ROBERT: Agreed! But my father was naturalized as French.

ROQUEFEUILLE: Just a minute! This is becoming serious. Was your father naturalized before or after your birth?

MAXIME: It was after.

ROBERT: That's possible, by a year or two, perhaps! I think I recall it was in the year that preceded our departure for Mauritius.

ROQUEFEUILLE: Then, my dear chap, don't go stand guard, you are not French.

ROBERT: What a joke! Am I Parisian?

ROQUEFEUILLE: You are Parisian, because you were born in Paris, that's evident; but you are English because your father was English at the moment of your birth. You are an English-Parisian, that's all, or a Parisian-English, as you like, it's all the same to me!

MAXIME: You see, you consult the law and the law replies to you.

ROBERT: Still—

ROQUEFEUILLE: Ah! I understand you! It seems strange that a kid of two years would have a definite personality; but your father who had a right to whip you, didn't have the right to confer nationality—that's all!

ROBERT: Goodness, goodness! This seems comical to me! I am English—Here I am English!

ROQUEFEUILLE: Perfectly right, sir.

ROBERT: That doesn't change me.

MAXIME: Want to see?

ROQUEFEUILLE: Want to see? You have absolutely the same head; only you are no longer a voter in France, nor fit for jury, nor the National Guard.

MAXIME: *(emphasizing)* Nor that National Guard!

ROBERT: I am no longer in The National Guard! I no longer mount my guard! Long Live John Bull! A cheer for John Bull!

ROQUEFEUILLE: I don't know your John Bull.

ROBERT: That doesn't signify—Hurrah! Hurrah! *(all three shout)*

MAXIME: Stop! Stop!

ROQUEFEUILLE: Ah, husband, go! If you are not French you are really worthy of being so!

ROBERT: *(noticing Laurence)* My wife! Heavens, indeed, now that I am English—Is she English, too?

ROQUEFEUILLE: Hush!

(Laurence enters.)

MAXIME: Ah, madame, we have a curious thing to impart to you.

ROBERT: *(low to Maxime)* Well, you aren't going—and my soiree?

MAXIME: Don't worry, I will stop in time.

LAURENCE: And me, I've got big news to announce to you.

ROBERT: I suspect yours is better than ours.

LAURENCE: You are going to judge.

ROQUEFEUILLE: Guess that your husband is?

LAURENCE: Is what?

ROBERT: *(low to Laurence)* The most repentant of men.

LAURENCE: The most certain of my forgiveness.

MAXIME: Why, no, why, no!

LAURENCE: Why, yes!

MAXIME: I mean to say that Robert has been deceived as to his nationality which is English. You've married an Englishman!

LAURENCE: Ah! An Englishman! What folly!

MAXIME: What do you think of my news?

LAURENCE: And you of mine: Leonie is in France!

MAXIME: Can it be true?

LAURENCE: Better still! She is here, and *(Leonie appears)* here she is!

MAXIME AND ROBERT: Madame de Vanvres!

ROQUEFEUILLE: As friend Maxime says: It's she.

LEONIE: Myself *(to Robert)* My dear Maubray! My dear Roquefeuille.

ROQUEFEUILLE: Ah, for goodness sake, now there's a pleasant surprise!

ROBERT: Be welcome, Madame.

LEONIE: I got in from Geneva just now, and, you see, my first visit is for my best friend.

LAURENCE: *(embracing her)* And your best friends thank you for it!

MAXIME: Not a word for me, madame?

LEONIE: Mr. Maxime, my intrepid traveler!

MAXIME: You didn't expect to see me again?

LEONIE: Why no, I assure you, and even—

MAXIME: What! Those words you deigned to pronounce one day? That promise of marriage?

LEONIE: Me marry, when I am free, independent? Oh! No, no!

ROQUEFEUILLE: *(to Maxime)* What was that you were telling me, you with your world tour?

MAXIME: But I thought—

ROQUEFEUILLE: A widow! A pussy cat—a scalded pussy cat!

LEONIE: What do you mean! He told you—ha, ha, ha—Imagine, that the first time chance threw us together was in Lisbon. We met as compatriots, and far from France, a compatriot is a bit of the country, and then at the first words exchanged, we suddenly found ourselves in the country of familiarity, we talked of you, of your husband, of notary, of Roquefeuille, I tell you—the next day.

ROBERT: The next day—

LEONIE: We shook hands like old friends, then the steamship took Mr. Duvernet to Rotterdam, and I took the flight to Algiers.

ROQUEFEUILLE: And that's all. A novel that stops after the first chapter?

MAXIME: No, indeed, that's not all! A year later, a new meeting at Vesuvius!

ROQUEFEUILLE: The Devil!

MAXIME: This time, I expressed to Madame all the passionate feelings that her sight gave birth to in me. I spoke to her of love, passion, fires, flames—she replied to me—

ROQUEFEUILLE: Volcano!

MAXIME: And the next day, a new departure, new separation!

LEONIE: Yes, but instead of taking the hand I offered him in friendship, didn't he have the audacity to ask for it?

LAURENCE: And you replied—?

MAXIME: Oh, an unheard of, strange, incredible thing! Madame replies that she has no time; but if chance reunited us somewhere for eleven days in Paris, she would give me the right to run around the world with her.

ALL: Eleven days!

MAXIME: You did say it?

LEONIE: Assuredly! Don't you know it takes eleven days to get married?

ROQUEFEUILLE: The fact is that if men were wise it would take eleven years.

MAXIME: Well, here we are in Paris, and—

LEONIE: Yes, but I'm leaving tomorrow.

MAXIME: Tomorrow!

(Baptiste brings in a platter with tea on it, places it on the table and leaves.)

LAURENCE: *(aside)* We will see about that.

LEONIE: My place is reserved at Havre, on the Panama, headed for Mauritius.

ALL: Mauritius!

MAXIME: And you believe that I will let you leave? No, madame; must I, in my capacity as doctor, poison the mate and the Captain of the Panama, it shall not leave!

LEONIE: Violence!

ROQUEFEUILLE: Yes, madam; it's been decided to quarantine all boats leaving France before eleven days have passed! Like the Duke of Buckingham!

MAXIME: And I will leave with you! Like it or not!

ROQUEFEUILLE: He's in his role! An absurd role, but he knows his part.

LEONIE: So as not to respond, I shall accept a cup of tea.

LAURENCE: Here it is, my dear Leonie.

MAXIME: For in the end your promises—Would you like some sugar?

LEONIE: Thanks!

ROBERT: *(to Roquefeuille, offering tea)* Marry!

ROQUEFEUILLE: Don't marry! Maxime: Your promises?

LEONIE: Yes, give me some cream.

ROBERT: Marry!

ROQUEFEUILLE: Don't marry!

LEONIE: Ah! While I'm thinking of it, my dear Maubray, I have a service to demand of you, a letter of recommendation! You probably know our French Counsel in Mauritius?

ROBERT: Perfectly! Monsieur de La Salle.

LEONIE: That's him indeed!

ROBERT: Do I know him! It was he who married us.

ROQUEFEUILLE: *(swallowing and choking)* Huh?

ROBERT: Well, what's the matter with him?

MAXIME: He's plotting mischief.

ROQUEFEUILLE: It was the French Consul who married you?

ROBERT: Yes. What of it?

ROQUEFEUILLE: Nothing to me? Oh! Nothing! Less than nothing!

LEONIE: What's wrong with him?

LAURENCE: He cannot hear of marriage without choking.

LEONIE: And now will you allow a little rest to a traveler who hasn't shut her eyes all night?

LAURENCE: It's not late! Eleven o'clock!

ROBERT: Eleven o'clock—and honor calls me to the flag! Let's go dress up in uniform, and wake to the Hail to the Empire.

MAXIME: Will you allow me, madame, to offer you my arm to your carriage?

LEONIE: At the moment it's only the arm that I accept. *(to Laurence)* Bye! *(hugging her)*

LAURENCE: Bye! Till tomorrow, right?

LEONIE: Till tomorrow! Well, Roquefeuille has become mute. Watch out! He's got some needle concealed under that rock.

ROQUEFEUILLE: Me, I—

LEONIE: We won't ask your secrets of you. Goodbye! *(She offers him her hand, Roquefeuille with a distracted air, gives her his tea-cup and notices her mirth. He confounds himself with excuses; Leonie, laughs, goes to Maxime.)*

MAXIME: *(low to Robert)* Decidedly, I am not going to Horace's place.

(Maxime leaves with Leonie.)

ROBERT: Goodnight, Roquefeuille. *(he speaks to his wife)* My darling Laurence, how bored I'm going to be far away from you!

(Robert kisses Laurence; she escorts him to the door. Roquefeuille who had taken a few steps, profits by the moment Laurence accompanies Robert to go into the other room to return and place his cane on the couch, and leaves on tip toe.)

LAURENCE: *(alone)* If my husband is bored on guard duty there will be sympathy between us at least.

ROQUEFEUILLE: *(entering at the back)* Where'd I put my cane?

LAURENCE: *(pointing the cane out to him)* There it is!

ROQUEFEUILLE: *(in a low voice)* I know that well enough!

LAURENCE: What do you mean?

ROQUEFEUILLE: Hush! *(he listens)* You cannot imagine the services this cane has rendered me in analogous circumstances.

LAURENCE: Ah, indeed! Explain to me—

ROQUEFEUILLE: Yes, I am going to explain the most singular fact, the most incredible, the most incomprehensible—the most—

LAURENCE: Hurry up indeed! Mr. de Sevigne!

ROQUEFEUILLE: First of all assure me that I am not deceiving myself. Allow me a question: we are alone?

LAURENCE: Absolutely alone! Speak quickly—You are beginning to frighten me.

ROQUEFEUILLE: You know what Mr. Duvernet told you as to the nationality of your husband? Of Robert, I mean?

LAURENCE: Why do you hesitate? Robert and my husband are one in the same!

ROQUEFEUILLE: A notary—allow me to resume my notary capacity for a moment—is held to the greatest rigor in the choice of his terms. So, I repeat, do you have Robert's birth certificate?

LAURENCE: It must be in his desk in his room.

ROQUEFEUILLE: Then would you go find it for me?

LAURENCE: But yet once more—

ROQUEFEUILLE: Do it, I beg you, my dear lady, what I ask of you; after that I will answer all your questions. Ah! Would you bring me your marriage certificate. *(Laurence leaves)* On honor! This will be very funny. But it's impossible; if Robert is unaware of it, the Consul must know the law.

LAURENCE: *(returning with a bunch of papers.)* Here's what I found.

ROQUEFEUILLE: Thanks! *(leafing through them)* Birth certificate. Naturalization papers. Maxime told the truth. Robert was two when his father was naturalized as French. Therefore, Robert is English. The marriage certificate! It really took place before the French Consul in Mauritius. But why didn't the Consul demand production of the birth certificate? Ah! Here it is! Robert appeared in the character of a French person, and the birth certificate, being in France was replaced by an affidavit of citizenship. *(aside)* Now I understand.

LAURENCE: Well! Am I to have the key to this enigma?

ROQUEFEUILLE: The key! You promise me you won't cry?

LAURENCE: Why no, my God!

ROQUEFEUILLE: And that you aren't going to faint?

LAURENCE: Ah! You are making me impatient! Speak quickly, I insist!

ROQUEFEUILLE: Well, miss—

LAURENCE: Miss!

ROQUEFEUILLE: You are not married.

LAURENCE: I am not married!

ROQUEFEUILLE: Your marriage is nul and void. Article 170—

LAURENCE: Nul and void!

ROQUEFEUILLE: *(shutting her mouth)* Hush! You promised not to scream!

LAURENCE: *(shaking)* Ah! My God!

ROQUEFEUILLE: You promised not to faint!

LAURENCE: It's not possible! You are playing with me. It's a shameful joke!

ROQUEFEUILLE: I never joke after midnight.

LAURENCE: Well then, don't tell me this! I am crazy to have listened to you for a single moment. You've got the proof of my marriage in your hands.

ROQUEFEUILLE: It's precisely because I have this proof in hand, that I repeat to you: "You are not married."

LAURENCE: Ah! For the last time!

ROQUEFEUILLE: The public officer was incompetent. It's as if you were married before a Forest Guard!

LAURENCE: *(losing her head)* Why, this is horrible! Why it's not my fault! But it's frightful! But, how was he able to do it?

ROQUEFEUILLE: Eh! My God! Quite simply! Robert thought he was French and he wasn't!

LAURENCE: Oh! My God, my god! Why what's going to become of me then? But I am not Robert's wife; I am only his—

ROQUEFEUILLE: Come on! Courage, calm down we will consider how to repair this. Happily, you have the entire night to consider.

LAURENCE: Yes, you are right; I'm going— *(Robert's voice is heard)*

ROQUEFEUILLE: Huh!

LAURENCE: *(terrified)* Robert's voice!

ROQUEFEUILLE: Already! Get hold of yourself and receive him!

LAURENCE: Oh! No.

ROQUEFEUILLE: What?

LAURENCE: Speak to him now! Why, am I able?

ROQUEFEUILLE: But, still—

LAURENCE: No, I don't wish to see him! My head is gone! I won't know what to say to him! He will guess everything. Oh! Why, no, I don't wish to see him!

ROQUEFEUILLE: But a husband—

LAURENCE: But is he my husband now? And think that—Ah, no indeed. *(She escapes to the right)*

ROQUEFEUILLE: *(perplexed)* Ah! That's right!

ROBERT: *(outside)* That's fine, that's fine—you can go to bed— *(Entering)* Heavens! you are still here, you?

ROQUEFEUILLE: Eh! Damn it! Yes—I've been looking for my cane for the last half hour. Where the devil did I hide my cane?

ROBERT: Why, there it is.

ROQUEFEUILLE: Heavens! It's true, there it is! Thanks! Goodnight!

ROBERT: Listen then!

ROQUEFEUILLE: Ah!! Yes, I really have time!

ROBERT: Two words!

ROQUEFEUILLE: Ta, ta, a rendez-vous. Someone's waiting for me, a romantic rendez-vous!

ROBERT: But—

ROQUEFEUILLE: Eh, you understand, I'm keeping my cane; a romantic rendez-vous, you never know what will happen; I'm keeping my cane. *(Roquefeuille goes to take his hat from the chimney.)*

ROBERT: That's my hat!

ROQUEFEUILLE: Ah! *(he puts it back and takes his own)*

ROBERT: And your cane?

ROQUEFEUILLE: I know where it is, that's all I need. Goodnight, and you, too! Thanks—Ouf! *(he escapes)*

ROBERT: Is he mad? Still, not as much as I am. How absurd we are! I told a lie to my wife, I deceived her for an hour of freedom, and no sooner was I at Horace's place than boredom took me by the throat and suffocated me. It's truly stupid, these bachelor meetings, and I don't understand how I was able. But repentance always follows sin, and I've come to confess everything. Laurence must be in her room and I— *(goes to open the door; it is locked; he raps, no response, astonished)* Ah! Locked!

CURTAIN

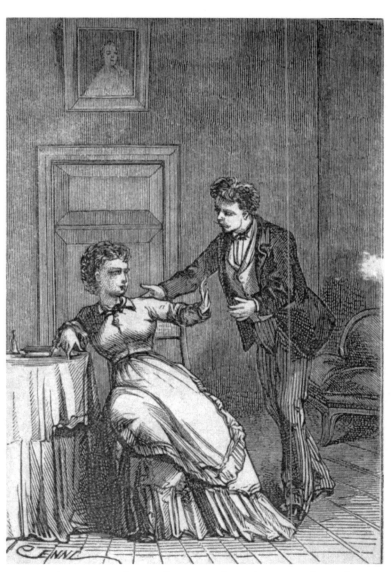

Act 2, *Eleven Days of Siege*, illustration from the 1878 Italian edition.

ACT II

LAURENCE: And so, even if I had children, the marriage would be nul and void?

ROQUEFEUILLE: Certainly. Their presence would have nothing to do with it; only the law which is strict, without being unjust, would recognize their rights as legitimate children.

LAURENCE: It's still the marriage which makes the children legitimate!

ROQUEFEUILLE: *(laughing)* Yes, more often than the husband!

LAURENCE: And there was no marriage?

ROQUEFEUILLE: Pardon me, there was one, but it no longer exists.

LAURENCE: It's true, you've explained it to me—good faith! Do you know, my poor Roquefeuille, that, if you had said nothing a week ago, I would still be married?

ROQUEFEUILLE: Ideally, yes, but in fact, no! And would you have preferred that Robert made this horrible discovery before you?

LAURENCE: Oh! No!

ROQUEFEUILLE: And the first discussion was a bit excited?

LAURENCE: *(exclaiming)* Oh!

ROQUEFEUILLE: Eh! my God! It's necessary to foresee and fear in this life! And foreseen in time, armed in war, with the enormous advantage of offensive, it belongs to us alone to avoid the peril even before it is suspected!

LAURENCE: That's right! You are a true friend, my dear Roquefeuille! You have no need of other papers than those I've delivered to you?

ROQUEFEUILLE: No!

LAURENCE: The publications?

ROQUEFEUILLE: Have been made.

LAURENCE: You have no other recommendations to—

ROQUEFEUILLE: You've suppressed the newspapers?

LAURENCE: Yes, but without knowing why.

ROQUEFEUILLE: I have my reasons: the press is so indiscreet. Did you see the man from city-hall yesterday?

LAURENCE: No!

ROQUEFEUILLE: Ah! In that case no one suspects anything?

LAURENCE: Yes, I thought it my duty to write to Leonie.

ROQUEFEUILLE: So much the worse!

LAURENCE: I am sure of her discretion.

ROQUEFEUILLE: I'd be even more sure of it if she knew nothing.

LAURENCE: It was bound to happen, my friend I had motives, reasons that I don't know how to explain to you.

ROQUEFEUILLE: That's different!

LAURENCE: Hush! It's she!

(Leonie enters.)

LEONIE: *(kissing Laurence)* Ah! My dear Laurence, my poor friend!

LAURENCE: Ah! My poor Leonie.

LEONIE: What! Yesterday, I left a married woman, and I find a young lady.

ROQUEFEUILLE: A widow, madame, —a deplorable widow!

LEONIE: Isn't this a mystification by this frightful notary? He's capable of anything.

LAURENCE: Alas, no!

LEONIE: And now it will last a week?

LAURENCE: A week!

LEONIE: And your husband knows nothing?

LAURENCE: Nothing.

LEONIE: And why haven't you confessed it to him?

ROQUEFEUILLE: I advised her to—but—

LAURENCE: I didn't dare.

LEONIE: Why?

LAURENCE: The evening in which Roquefeuille informed me of the fatal secret, Robert spent the night out. I was counting then on having some hours to reflect on my strange position and the new duties that it imposed on me when I heard the voice of my husband; my first, my only idea was to rush into my room and barricade myself inside.

LEONIE: Ah!

ROQUEFEUILLE: *(aside)* And to say that Robert didn't break down the door! Clumsy! Violence with his wife would have been delicious!

LAURENCE: My God! after having rapped several times, seeing that I didn't answer, he took the role of retiring. As for me, I didn't close my eye all night; the most crazy ideas succeeded one another in my head, and I wasn't able to see clearly in the chaos when day came. I rose, not knowing what part to take, almost confiding my destiny to chance or to the inspiration of the moment. I met Robert, and already my secret rose to my lips, when his cold and severe air stopped it. For my wrongs, was he angry with me when he woke up, was he after me because of my shut door on his return? I don't know but I found him so cold, so severe—I remained trembling, my heart was palpitating—I saw only dangers in speaking. I kept my secret, and since that moment, each day augments my embarrassment and diminishes my courage!

LEONIE: But what do you fear?

LAURENCE: Do I know? You know my husband, he's neither better nor worse than anyone else, indeed he has ideas a little cruel about things of this world. But, say to most husbands after three years of marriage: You are free!

ROQUEFEUILLE: Ah what a stroke! How to save yourself if you can!

LEONIE: The gentleman is exaggerating. Many would resume the road to city-hall.

ROQUEFEUILLE: Yes—with other women!

LAURENCE: *(to Leonie)* You see how reassuring he is! And perhaps he's right, my dear. Robert loves me, I think—he's a man of honor, I am sure; but after three years of marriage isn't it like a tree which has given all its flowers, all its fruits—and that one sees fall without regret? Why risk all my happiness on a word?

LEONIE: But this silence cannot last forever. What will be the end of this comedy?

ROQUEFEUILLE: The end of all comedies: a marriage!

LAURENCE: Here's what Roquefeuille has advised me: Keep my secret quiet for eleven days.

LEONIE: Eleven days—the time necessary.

ROQUEFEUILLE: For publications, yes. —And during this time, let me do the needful things, furnish the papers, publish the bans, etc. The Mayor of our district is my friend, which simplifies things.

LEONIE: And the eleventh day?

ROQUEFEUILLE: The eleventh day, escort Robert to city-hall, under some sort of pretext, still without telling him anything, and there—abruptly inform him of the truth.

LEONIE: Just like that, all of a sudden?

ROQUEFEUILLE: That's it!

LEONIE: What's the advantage?

ROQUEFEUILLE: Immense! So as not to give him time to reflect—

LEONIE: Why, it's—

ROQUEFEUILLE: It's a trap, I'm perfectly aware; but it's the only way to get there! Because if one gives him eleven days to consider—Oh!

LEONIE: What a monster this notary is!

ROQUEFEUILLE: Yes, but what a notary this monster is!

LAURENCE: In short! All is agreed in a way, and I only regret not having a mother, a sister, with whom I could retire during this time, under the first pretext that came.

LEONIE: Why? Aren't you comfortable here?

ROQUEFEUILLE: Yes! This young girl's scruple seems a bit late to me!

LAURENCE: This is none of your concern, my dear Roquefeuille, these are feminine secrets that your ears cannot understand, —and if you were really nice—

ROQUEFEUILLE: Very nice! Your servant, Roquefeuille!

LAURENCE: Oh! My friend—

ROQUEFEUILLE: Good! Good! I'll go into Robert's room.

LAURENCE: Thanks!

ROQUEFEUILLE: You can talk without fear. You know I am not forgetting my cane. *(he leaves)*

LEONIE: Well, what did you want to say?

LAURENCE: See what this strange situation has done to me: since I've known the nullity of my marriage, I am no longer of good faith, I no longer have the right to consider myself as married—

LEONIE: Well?

LAURENCE: All the while my husband, whose ignorance assures his good faith, still thinks himself—

LEONIE: What, you are making a serious case of this to the point of --

LAURENCE: But, in the end, think that I am not married!—and I don't know what any other woman would do in my place—; as for me, at the risk of seeming a bit ridiculous, I confess to you that one scruple—bizarre perhaps—an exaggerated delicacy it's possible—but still no!—No!—No!—

LEONIE: And what does your husband say?

LAURENCE: He doesn't say anything.

LEONIE: He's really quite angry?

LAURENCE: I thought he was the first day, I told you, but the same evening his bad humor disappeared, and disappeared so completely that my situation has become very difficult—

LEONIE: What! For a week—you retire each night into your fortifications?

LAURENCE: Yes.

LEONIE: And Mr. Maubray to his camp?

LAURENCE: Yes.

LEONIE: And except for covering fire, all communication is interrupted between the two places?

LAURENCE: Yes.

LEONIE: Ah, indeed, ah! Why, now there's a delicate situation!

LAURENCE: Even more delicate because during the day, I make myself as sweet, as friendly, as attentive as possible!

LEONIE: You come out from your fortifications?

LAURENCE: And at night—

LEONIE: You return to your lines?

LAURENCE: You said it.

LEONIE: And the besieger?

LAURENCE: *(lowering her eyes)* Ah! Sometimes he's in a very bad mood!

LEONIE: Hell! He's within his rights to be.

LAURENCE: Why that's exactly what scares me; it's precisely for that I need your help!

LEONIE: Speak!

(Baptiste enters with a newspaper in his hand.)

LAURENCE: What do you want?

BAPTISTE: These are the newspapers that I am bringing to the master.

LAURENCE: Put them there!

BAPTISTE: But, madame, the master is accustomed—

LAURENCE: That's fine I tell you; put them there!

(Baptiste leaves.)

LEONIE: What do you intend to do with these newspapers?

LAURENCE: It's Roquefeuille who advised me to suppress them with the greatest care.

LEONIE: And why?

LAURENCE: I don't know.

LEONIE: Ah, the publications, no question—*(She takes a paper; Laurence takes the other papers and puts them into a little furniture at the right.)*

LAURENCE: You are right.

LEONIE: Let's see— *(reading)* Paris First—Miscellanies: That's not it. Ah! Marriage Banns: Between Mr.Lenormand, 5 rue Coquilliere, and Miss Danjou, same house. Mr. de Valois, Rue Royale, and Miss Laurence, same house—

LAURENCE: Why always: same house?

LEONIE: I don't see why—Ah! Here!

LAURENCE: Continue!

LEONIE: Mr. Robert Maubray, 8 rue de Londres, and Miss Laurence de Croix— *(Leonie gives her the paper)*

LAURENCE: *(reading)* Same house!

LEONIE: Now do you understand?

LAURENCE: Ah! Yes—Watch out! My husband—*(hiding the paper)*

ROBERT: *(aside)* Always with someone! *(aloud)* Madame!

LEONIE: My dear Maubray!

ROBERT: You are very scarce; we almost never see you.

LEONIE: You are very good to notice that.

ROBERT: And you, my dear Laurence, this neuralgia?

LEONIE: A neuralgia?

LAURENCE: *(to Robert)* Still suffering, my friend.

ROBERT: Take care of yourself. You know how dear your health is to me! *(going to kiss her)*

LAURENCE: *(crying)* Oh! Be careful!

ROBERT: *(in a bad mood)* It's astonishing how this neuralgia persists! You haven't seen my newspapers?

LAURENCE: *(hiding them behind her)* No!

ROBERT: It's strange; this has been happening to me for two or three days already! Madame! *(to himself)* Oh! This neuralgia! Absolutely, I must know what's become of them! *(exit Robert)*

LAURENCE: *(after having assured herself of Robert's departure resumes reading the paper)* Mr. Robert Maubray, 8 rue de Londres, and Miss La Croix, same house. There it is. Ah:—Mr. Maxime Duvernet 17, rue Louis le Grand, and Madame de Vanvres—

LEONIE: *(taking the paper)* What! I am in it; we are in it! Ah ! Mr. Duvernet hasn't declared himself beaten! He keeps it up! He intends to marry me despite myself.

LAURENCE: He loves you, that's his excuse.

LEONIE: Well, he will lose his expenses; for this morning I received a letter from Havre that informs me that the Panama is leaving in three days.

LAURENCE: You are going?

LEONIE: Do you want me to marry this gentleman?

LAURENCE: I want—I want you to stay.

LEONIE: Then you don't understand that if I stay, I will be here, quite simply eleven days and I—

LAURENCE: You don't understand that if you leave, I am ruined?

LEONIE: Ruined!

LAURENCE: Yes, ruined! Robert was astonished at first, then uneasy in the new position made for him. It was really necessary to invent something—I invented—

LEONIE: Ah! Yes, neuralgia

LAURENCE: But, now—

LEONIE: He believes you less?

LAURENCE: He doesn't believe me at all!

LEONIE: The drama is getting complicated.

LAURENCE: And the siege continues! And I am losing ground by the moment! And the fort must be held for three days more you understand, three days? I am lost if you do not come to my assistance.

LEONIE: How?

LAURENCE: You must renounce your departure so as to come live in this house and not leave me!

LEONIE: Oh! Oh! Oh!

LAURENCE: You are hesitating?

LEONIE: Well, I should think so! And then if this comedy drags out a bit longer it's my liberty itself which finds itself compromised, without speaking of the abominable rancor that Mr. Maubray is going to devote to me.

LAURENCE: You refuse?

LEONIE: Why, hell! Think about it—Well, no! It shall not be said in future ages that Madame de Vanvres refused reinforcements to her best friend! I will enter your home with arms and baggage, we will resupply the fort, and all is saved, even honor!

LAURENCE: Ah! How good you are! *(kissing her)*

LEONIE: Now there's a kiss I would never have stolen!

(Enter Maxime.)

BAPTISTE: *(announcing)* Mr. Duvernet!

MAXIME: Madame!

LAURENCE: Pardon me, Maxime, if I leave you so precipitously!

MAXIME: Madame!

LEONIE: We have some arrangements to take—

MAXIME: She, too?

THE TWO WOMEN: And we present you our very humble excuses. *(They leave)*

MAXIME: Now there's a woman who will make me damned before marriage!

ROQUEFEUILLE: *(entering)* There are some folks in a big hurry!

ROBERT: *(entering)* Ah! Maxime! By Jove! I was going to send to your place! Are we alone?

ROQUEFEUILLE: Yes.

ROBERT: Well, I am delighted to have both of you two! I have to consult you.

MAXIME: As a doctor?

ROQUEFEUILLE: As a notary? Or as friend?

ROBERT: As friends above all! As notary, perhaps! But especially as doctor!

ROQUEFEUILLE: It's Panurge's consultation?

ROBERT: And on the same question, marriage!

ROQUEFEUILLE: Only Panurge was more clever; he consulted in advance.

MAXIME: We are listening to you, speak!

ROBERT: As friends, first of all. Imagine that a mystery has reigned in this house for a week that I've vainly tried to penetrate. My wife is no longer the same; she flees me; she avoids me. Nothing works as it used to; there are continual comings and goings of folks I don't know. Yesterday, a very ill dressed gentleman came to offer the services of his administration, and after a long conversation it was only a question of city-hall, of a ceremonial carriage, etc, I thought I understood it was a question of burial.

MAXIME: Heavens!

ROQUEFEUILLE: And you didn't profit by the opportunity?

ROBERT: And that's not all! My wife locks herself up for hours to read, and do you know what novel I found on her desk? The Civil Code—opened on the chapter on marriage—The respective rights of spouses.

ROQUEFEUILLE: Ah! That's curious—was there a book mark?

ROBERT: Bad joke! In the end, not even my newspapers can I lay my hands for the past week.

ROQUEFEUILLE: Strange! Strange!

MAXIME: And your conclusion?

ROBERT: Yours is?

ROQUEFEUILLE: You have no other indications?

ROBERT: Yes, there are others, but—

MAXIME: But—?

ROBERT: It's delicate to discuss!

MAXIME: You can say anything to your notary.

ROQUEFEUILLE: And to your doctor.

ROBERT: Well, so be it! You plainly see this door?

MAXIME: I see it.

ROBERT: It's the door to my wife's room.

MAXIME: Well?

ROBERT: Well, do me the pleasure of opening it?

MAXIME: Huh?

ROBERT: Do it anyway!

ROQUEFEUILLE: Open the door for him for the love of God!

MAXIME: *(going to the door to the right)* So be it!—Locked!

ROBERT: Well, yes, locked! But locked as one does not lock a door, especially to a husband! So, that's what it's been like for a week.

ROQUEFEUILLE AND MAXIME: *(laughing)* Ah, bah!

ROBERT: I will admit to you, my dear friends, that your laughter irritates me!

ROQUEFEUILLE: What! It's not even open at the discreet hour when Psyche extinguishes her lamp?

ROBERT: No!

ROQUEFEUILLE: Well, what do you want us to do about it, my poor friend? We really, cannot—

ROBERT: By Jove! I know that well enough! But I want advice— some good advice!

MAXIME: What advice?

ROBERT: That of a Notary, first of all!

ROQUEFEUILLE: Go ahead!

ROBERT: Does my wife have the right to refuse me?

ROQUEFEUILLE: Obedience? No! Article 213—

ROBERT: Have I the right to demand—

ROQUEFEUILLE: Obedience? Yes! Same article 213.

ROBERT: Fine! So I'm at ease on the subject of legality!

ROQUEFEUILLE: You can sue your wife in court for that

ROBERT: No, no, no! Only, I know my right. That's immense!

ROQUEFEUILLE: Keep going! You will amuse yourself infinitely.

ROBERT: *(to Maxime)* You understand well enough that I am not easily resigned to this role of—

MAXIME: Of Tantalus?

ROBERT: Of Tantalus, so be it! And that I've asked my wife the cause of this anticipated divorce—

MAXIME: And she replied to you that she was ill?

ROBERT: That she was ill—with nerves

ROQUEFEUILLE AND MAXIME: With nerves.

ROBERT: With nerves!

MAXIME: Well, that reason is better than another!

ROBERT: The reason is pitiful, my dear chap. Laurence has never had greater appearance of the most magnificent health. She is as fresh as at fifteen, and pretty as a cherub.

ROQUEFEUILLE: You are looking at her through the eyes of a bachelor.

MAXIME: Look, let's be serious! Do you know you've done something wrong? Is your wife angry with you?

ROBERT: No, indeed! And the proof is that during the day she is charming, almost flirtatious with me; but as the Sun descends on the horizon—

MAXIME: The beauties of the day lock themselves in bed with the Sun! And this began—

ROBERT: The day my guard letter came, you remember—that curious discovery of my nationality.

MAXIME: *(laughing)* By Jove! Now there's the reason! No need to seek others! She wants to break off all relations with you—because you are English.

ROQUEFEUILLE: Oh! Oh! Oh! At the moment of the treaty of commerce? Not likely?

ROBERT: *(impatiently)* My God! You joke about it!

MAXIME: Seriously, I'm distracted by it!

ROBERT: I have only one resource, it's to address myself to you, my friend. I want you, adroitly, without Laurence suspecting it, for you to tell me if my wife is ill, yes or no.

MAXIME: What! Without her suspecting it? Why, miscreant, have you considered that for us doctors the only thermometers are the pulse and the tongue?

ROQUEFEUILLE: And if she doesn't lend herself to it?

MAXIME: If she mustn't suspect?

ROBERT: Ta, ta, ta, manage it your own way; find some clever means, deviously, to reach your end.

MAXIME: But—

ROQUEFEUILLE: Hush! The door is opening.

MAXIME: It's broad day light!

ROBERT: Here's my wife; I am leaving you with her. Come, Roquefeuille.

MAXIME: No, by Jove! Much better for you to be here!

ROQUEFEUILLE: *(aside)* And me, too!

LAURENCE: *(entering)* You don't wish me ill for it, Maxime, for having left you alone for a moment?

MAXIME: Robert kept me company.

ROQUEFEUILLE: *(aside)* Careful! Roquefeuille—warn her *(Low to Laurence)* Be—

LAURENCE: Huh?

ROQUEFEUILLE: Me? *(coughing)* Ah, my friends, I think I've got the grip.

MAXIME: But what I don't forgive you for, Madame, is for having carried off Madame de Vanvres, if I weren't certain it was to prevent her departure.

LAURENCE: Exactly!

ROQUEFEUILLE: *(same as before)* Be careful!

LAURENCE: You were saying?

ROQUEFEUILLE: *(pretending to think she's interrupted Robert)* You said?

ROBERT: As for me, I didn't breathe a word.

ROQUEFEUILLE: *(to Laurence)* He didn't breathe a word.

LAURENCE: Ah! I thought *(aside)* What's the matter with them anyway?

ROBERT: *(low to Maxime)* Go to it!

LAURENCE: And of what were you speaking when I interrupted your conversation? Is there anything indiscreet about asking you?

MAXIME: *(aside)* How to manage it?

ROQUEFEUILLE: *(aside)* Let's see how to get her out of it?

MAXIME: *(aloud)* Ah! Yes, madame, I was telling these gentlemen some particulars of my voyages. I said that Europe, which thinks itself the head of civilization, has been outdistanced in certain sciences by the natives of Oceania. In divination, for example.

LAURENCE: In divination!

ROQUEFEUILLE: *(aside)* Now there's a devious means.

LAURENCE: You believe in that science?

MAXIME: Yes, madame; but I make an extreme difference between the science of Mr. Desbarolles and that of the inhabitants of Nouka-Hiva.

ROBERT: *(low)* Indeed.

MAXIME: Example: palm reading.

ROQUEFEUILLE: Ah! There it is!

MAXIME: *(continuing)* Palm reading can, at most, reveal the past. May I have your hand, if you please.

ROQUEFEUILLE: *(low to Laurence)* No, don't give it!

LAURENCE: My hand!

ROBERT: *(aside)* Finally!

ROQUEFEUILLE: No, don't give it! *(low)*

LAURENCE: *(not comprehending)* But—

ROBERT: Give your hand, dear friend!

ROQUEFEUILLE: *(aside)* Then there is only one way. *(to Laurence)* Give me your other.

MAXIME: *(low to Robert)* Take your watch and count one minute.

ROBERT: I understand!

MAXIME: Hand of a thoroughbred, Madame. Hum!

ROQUEFEUILLE: *(taking her other hand)* Completely aristocratic. *(Robert counts and looks at Roquefeuille)*

MAXIME: Well, what's he doing?

ROQUEFEUILLE: I am making a counter-test.

LAURENCE: Explain this to me?

ROQUEFEUILLE: We are going to tell you your good fortune, beautiful lady. Let it be done!

ROBERT: *(low to Maxime)* Count!

MAXIME: Well, Madame, you have a long hand, slender fingers—twenty—

ROQUEFEUILLE: Forty!

MAXIME: And what we call the psychic hand—forty.

ROQUEFEUILLE: Eighty!

MAXIME: Which ought to marvelously serve the conceptions of a superior intelligence.

ROBERT: *(low to Maxime)* That's it!

MAXIME: *(low)* Sixty pulsations! Pulse is excellent!

ROQUEFEUILLE: That's it, 120! A horse fever!

ROBERT: What?

ROQUEFEUILLE: A horse fever!

ROBERT: You are crazy or your watch doesn't work!

ROQUEFEUILLE: My watch doesn't work? My mother's watch!

ROBERT: Go to the devil! Let's see the tongue! *(aside)* Oof! And what a one! *(to Laurence)* Oh! You are not done yet, madame—it seems that it's not over.

LAURENCE: What's this all about?

MAXIME: In the art of divination, madame, the hand is only the first page of the book!

LAURENCE: What is the second?

MAXIME: It's—don't laugh in advance—it's the tongue!

ROQUEFEUILLE: *(to Laurence)* Close your mouth!

ROBERT: Ah! As to that, you'll never persuade me!

MAXIME: And why not? Isn't the tongue the virtual expression of our thoughts? All our organs obey our will, the tongue alone is indispensable, and as a starter, doesn't know how to lie, physically, of course! They say: a long tongue for a person clever and witty, a thick tongue for a moron and an imbecile.

ROQUEFEUILLE: And a well hung tongue on a gossiper.

MAXIME: Yes!

ROQUEFEUILLE: Yes!

MAXIME: And what's astonishing about observant people who have made the tongue the mirror of the future?

ROBERT: I give up! I give up! And, if Laurence will indeed loan herself—

LAURENCE: What, sir, you want— *(laughing)* Ah! This can't be serious?

ROQUEFEUILLE: Close your mouth! *(She closes her lips)*

ROBERT: I beg your pardon, nothing is more serious!

LAURENCE: Ah! For goodness sakes! *(she laughs)*

ROQUEFEUILLE: *(putting his pince nez on his nose)* Come on, beautiful lady, come on, put out your tongue!

LAURENCE: *(breaking into laughter)* Ah! My word! I cannot! Ha, ha, ha! *(she falls laughing onto the sofa. Maxime and Robert look at her, as Roquefeuille sticks his tongue out at them.)*

ROBERT: Didn't make it!

MAXIME: *(to Roquefeuille)* It's your fault!

ROQUEFEUILLE: Mine?

MAXIME AND ROBERT: Yes, you made her laugh!

ROQUEFEUILLE: It was you!

MAXIME AND ROBERT: It was you!

ROQUEFEUILLE: It was you.

LEONIE: *(entering)* My God! What's the matter?

LAURENCE: Ah! The most clownish idea!

MAXIME: *(quickly)* It's nothing. *(aside)* Not much more was needed to make me ridiculous in her eyes?

LEONIE: My room is ready; do you want to give the order to your servants to bring my baggage?

MAXIME: Servants? Ah, madame—no other than myself is necessary.

ROQUEFEUILLE: And me? *(aside)* Let's call off the hounds!

LEONIE: Ah! You are very gallant, the two of you! Well, follow me!

MAXIME: To the end of the world!

ROQUEFEUILLE: *(low, to Laurence)* Oof! And by two! But watch out for that guy, he has some ideas—flighty ones. *(he escapes)*

ROBERT: *(as Leonie, Maxime and Roquefeuille leave)* My wife says she's ill, and is marvelously well! We are really going to see! You are fleeing me, Laurence?

LAURENCE: Me?

ROBERT: Stay, I beg you—you'd think I frighten you.

LAURENCE: Oh!

ROBERT: And, I confess, I myself, am tempted to believe it a little, to see the care with which you avoid me.

LAURENCE: I avoid you?

ROBERT: I don't suppose you will say that it's chance alone which is putting a third party in our private conversation, and ceaselessly raises a barrier between the two of us?

LAURENCE: Why, yes, truly—I haven't noticed—

ROBERT: You cannot know, my dear Laurence, the pleasure that you give me in speaking this way; for, on honor, I had almost begun to suspect your affection.

LAURENCE: Oh, Robert, what an idea!

ROBERT: Ah! Damn, dear friend, you know, the heart can become tired, in the end, of loving alone, of struggling alone, and without another heart to respond to it, and then—Come sit near me.

LAURENCE: (terrified) Thanks! Thanks!

ROBERT: Again! You move away when I call you?

LAURENCE: I am not moving away! (she recoils)

ROBERT: Then come, I beg you.

LAURENCE: (sitting) Got to do it!

ROBERT: Ah! And now, my dear Laurence, that we are, one on one with each other, no longer old spouses, but like young lovers, will you tell me what is the subject of your preoccupations?

LAURENCE: I assure you—

ROBERT: Haven't we been living like strangers for the past week?

LAURENCE: (wishing to rise) Robert!

ROBERT: There! See, the very moment in which for the first time, I find you alone, you already want to leave me. You don't love me.

LAURENCE: I don't love you! *(aside)* What torture!

ROBERT: Is this a young girl? Is this my wife who is speaking to me?

LAURENCE: *(aside)* Oh! My God!

ROBERT: I would understand you if you were Miss de Croix instead of being Madame Maubray, and if my passion—

LAURENCE: Why, I assure you there's nothing to it, I—

ROBERT: If you loved me would your eyes be lowering themselves before mine? If you loved me, would you find me ridiculous and boring? If you loved me, would you push away my arm which entwines your waist? *(he takes her by the waist)*

LAURENCE: *(overwhelmed by agitation)* Robert! Robert!

ROBERT: As for me, I love you! *(he wants to take her in his arms, she rises)*

LEONIE: *(entering with a hatbox)* It's only me, dear friends, don't be disturbed!

ROBERT: Plague on all intruders!

LEONIE: *(low to Laurence)* It seems I got here just in time!

ROBERT: How did it happen my dear Laurence, that your servants didn't announce Madame de Vanvres?

LEONIE: What do you mean, announce me? They won't announce me now that I am part of the household.

ROBERT: Of the household?

LEONIE: Why, you see plainly, I am moving in.

ROBERT: What! That room you were speaking of?

LEONIE: Why, it's here!

ROBERT: Here!

LEONIE: Your wife didn't tell you? Because she wanted to give you a pleasant surprise!

ROBERT: *(aside)* She's giving herself a bodyguard!

LEONIE: *(low to Laurence)* He's furious!

LAURENCE: You're not miffed with me, my friend, for what I've done?

ROBERT: Not at all! I am enchanted, enchanted!

LEONIE: I told these gentlemen to put my effects in my room.

ROBERT: The guest room at the other end of the apartment?

LEONIE: What are you thinking of? A place inhabited by all sorts of people? I would die the first night. No, no, the room adjoining that of your wife. *(starts to leave)*

ROBERT: *(furious)* Say her room right out, and let's not speak of it anymore! *(to Laurence)* Finally, as I was telling you, my dear Laurence—

LEONIE: Over here, Mr. Maxime, this way!

MAXIME: *(enters, with irony)* Here I am, madame!

ROBERT: *(walking around agitatedly)* The other one! Ah! They are pushing things to extremes!

MAXIME: What's the matter with him?

LEONIE: He's got the vapors. Well, my hat boxes, and my dresses, and Mr. Roquefeuille.

ROQUEFEUILLE: *(entering with boxes)* Here, here, here!

ROBERT: Again! It only lacked him!

LEONIE: This way, gentlemen!

ROQUEFEUILLE: *(unburdening himself)* Oof! And they want me to get married!

ROBERT: *(aside)* Come on! It's over! I am no longer in my own home! It's a train station, a loading platform! Oh! I'd enjoy breaking something. *(he rings)*

LAURENCE: *(low to Leonie)* How will this end?

BAPTISTE: *(entering)* Monsieur rang?

ROBERT: My papers!

BAPTISTE: Why, sir—

ROBERT: I asked you for my newspapers! Is that clear?

BAPTISTE: It's that—

ROBERT: You don't reply: it's that—to a man who asks for his newspapers. If my papers don't get here by tomorrow, you will be discharged—

LAURENCE: They mis-sent it my friend. *(to Robert)* Go, and keep your mouth shut! *(he leaves)*

ROQUEFEUILLE: *(to Robert)* For the last week, nothing but platitudes in the papers.

ROBERT: How much patience one must have!

MAXIME: *(laughing)* And all that because you haven't read your paper. You can boast of being a proud original!

ROBERT: Does that concern you? Yes, I am furious because papers do not vanish without a trace! For the last week I haven't seen a single one!

MAXIME: If that's what's bothering you, see the lucky chance! I can come to your assistance.

ROQUEFEUILLE: Huh!

MAXIME: I've got today's newspaper in my pocket!

LAURENCE: *(aside)* Ah!

LEONIE: *(aside)* Clumsy!

ROQUEFEUILLE: He really needed it!

ROBERT: At bottom, I don't care much about it.

MAXIME: Yes, yes! There's a story in it which concerns me, and under the title of friend, you ought to be interested in it.

ROQUEFEUILLE: *(low to Maxime)* Be quiet, will you?

LEONIE: *(low)* Be quiet, will you?

MAXIME: Huh? Is it wrong to say, madame, that your name appears near mine in the publication.

LEONIE: For certain, sir, you will compromise me.

LAURENCE: *(low to Roquefeuille)* He's going to see ours, too!

ROQUEFEUILLE: By Jove! How to parry the blow?

ROBERT: Ah! Ah! You are there already? My compliments—

ROQUEFEUILLE: My condolences!

LEONIE: *(getting between Maxime and Robert)* Don't read it! I never authorized Mr. Duvernet—don't read it!

ROBERT: Indeed! Indeed!

LAURENCE: What to do?

LEONIE: *(low to Roquefeuille)* On guard! *(Robert reads the paper)*

ROQUEFEUILLE: Some cool headedness! Some audacity! *(to Leonie)* What are you looking for, madame? A piece of cardboard or some paper to divide this linen?

LEONIE: Yes, exactly.

ROQUEFEUILLE: *(in a low voice)* The newspaper?

LEONIE: Understood?

ROBERT: Where are these publications that I cannot find?

MAXIME: On the fourth page!—Dummy!

ROBERT: That's right!

LEONIE: *(taking the paper)* Excuse me, my dear Maubray, now this is what we need.

LAURENCE: Oh!

ROQUEFEUILLE: Well executed!

ROBERT: *(astonished, containing himself)* Why, madame you don't use a whole newspaper, to divide a skein of linen!

LEONIE: That's perfectly true! You see, when I am wrong, I admit it. *(she tears the paper in two and gives him the first half)* Here, read your Paris first.

ROQUEFEUILLE: *(aside)* Bravo! And they want me to get married? Ah, no!

MAXIME: *(going to Leonie and taking half of the paper)* No indeed, no indeed, madame! The paragraph that I want to make Robert read is in the second part of the paper.

LEONIE: *(low)* My God, how impossible you are!

MAXIME: You are saying?

LEONIE: I said nothing.

MAXIME: I heard wrong.

ROQUEFEUILLE: Animal!

MAXIME: Huh? *(he takes half of the paper, tears it in two and returns half to Leonie)* There's still enough there to divide ten skeins! *(to Robert)* And if you wish to cast your eyes— *(he gives him a quarter of the paper)*

ROBERT: *(Aside, looking at Leonie)* Now there's a little lady who will quite simply make me commit a crime. *(taking the paper from Maxime)* Give it to me.

LAURENCE: *(to Roquefeuille)* Lost!

ROQUEFEUILLE: *(low)* Not yet! *(he turns over the ink on the table)* Ah!

LAURENCE: Ah!

MAXIME: What's the matter?

ROBERT: It seems it is not over.

ROQUEFEUILLE: Ah! My God! Madame has just overturned the ink and made an enormous spot on the table. It's the Black

Sea. How to repair it? Quick, madame a scrap of paper!

THE WOMEN: Ah! My God! It's spreading! Quickly.

ROQUEFEUILLE: *(slowly takes the leaf which Robert was holding and gives it to Leonie.)* Here, Madame, dry! Dry!

LEONIE: Let's dry it. *(she rubs with the paper)*

LAURENCE: Just in time!

MAXIME: Why, madame, for the love of God!

LEONIE: Meddle with what concerns you, my dear sir.

MAXIME: But—

ROBERT: *(to Leonie)* Ah, indeed! Madame, are you making fun of me, by chance?

LEONIE: Can you think that? I assure you that it doesn't appear so; but I am desolated—

ROQUEFEUILLE: It doesn't appear so at all.

ROBERT: Eh! It's really a question of this table!

LEONIE: Then what is it a question of? This is not a scrap of paper, I suppose?

ROBERT: Indeed, madame.

LEONIE: That's right? That's the one you were reading? How stupid you are, Roquefeuille!

ROQUEFEUILLE: It's me then—But the injury can be repaired. Could I suspect that they attached so much importance to a nasty end of a newspaper? In what condition is it now?

MAXIME: Here it is, but in a pitiful state.

ROQUEFEUILLE: It's slightly stained, but with a little good will—

MAXIME: Impossible to decipher a line.

LAURENCE: *(low to Leonie)* I am saved.

ROBERT: *(to Leonie, explosively)* Madame!

LEONIE: My God! What's the matter with him?

ROBERT: *(beside himself)* So, madame, I am not duped by all this! This paper is only a pretext for the continual persecutions of which I am the object! I don't know what bad wind has blown through my household, but for a week, that is to say, since your arrival, everything here has gone from bad to worse. My wife forgets that she is my wife, my friends forget they are my friends! I don't dare affirm that this is all your work—

LEONIE: But you believe it?

ROBERT: But I believe it.

LEONIE: That's frank at least.

MAXIME: Robert.

LAURENCE: My friend!

ROBERT: Leave me alone! Because you are all in agreement! Leave me!

LAURENCE: What do you intend to do?

ROBERT: Oh! Nothing, I don't even want to impose the sacrifice of a friend, and I am giving up the territory. *(he leaves)*

MAXIME: Robert! Robert!

(Robert has shut the door in her face. Maxime leaves by the back left. Music until the lowering of the curtain.)

ROQUEFEUILLE: Well!

LEONIE: Well!

LAURENCE: Well!

ROQUEFEUILLE: As Pyrhhus would have said, another victory like that and it's over for us!

LEONIE: We were pushing things a bit far!

LAURENCE: Ah! I feel it indeed! But what to do now?

LEONIE: Damn!

ROQUEFEUILLE: There can be no hesitation. You must make peace, fast! Fast!

LAURENCE: And how to make peace?

ROQUEFEUILLE: That's your affair! When a place under siege cannot defend itself, it hoists up a flag and capitulates! Capitulate!

LEONIE: Yes, capitulate! Capitulate!

LAURENCE: *(heading towards Robert's door)* Indeed, you are right! What have I gained by this comedy? Today, the wrath, perhaps tomorrow, the indifference of Robert. I've compromised my happiness too much already.

ROQUEFEUILLE: *(at the back)* Capitulate!

LEONIE: Capitulate!

LAURENCE: *(going to Robert's door and trying to open it)* Locked.

ROQUEFEUILLE: *(to Leonie)* Locked!

ALL THREE: Ah!

CURTAIN

ACT III

LEONIE: Well, what news?

MAXIME: None!

LEONIE: None!

MAXIME: Nothing. I just left the prefecture of police, they asked me a thousand questions. I told them all that I knew: that our friend Robert was a little fantastic; that after a lively enough scene, he withdrew to his room; that the same evening his wife found his door locked; that the next day, not seeing him appear, it was decided to break down the door; that the room

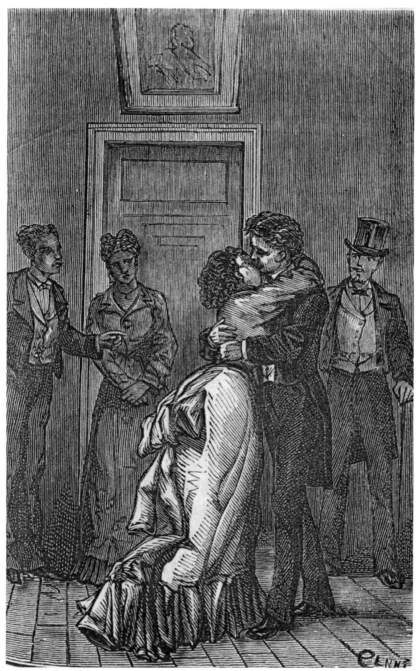

Act 3, *Eleven Days of Siege*, illustration from the 1878 Italian edition,
Courtesy Volker Dehs Collection.

was empty, and that our friend left by his private stairway, and that since then, he hasn't been seen at home, nor at his club, nor on the exchange—and finally that his wife was mortally uneasy.

LEONIE: I really think so!

MAXIME: All that was written swiftly by a bearded gentleman who dismissed me with these words: "That's fine, sir, we'll find him—" And I came hastily to give an account of my actions, while Roquefeuille rushed to Chatou to see if he isn't in his country house.

LEONIE: What an event! This disappearance! This flight!

MAXIME: And now, madame, that I've done what friendship demanded of me, will I be permitted not to neglect love completely, and to cause you to notice that we are today, precisely at that famous eleventh day which must never shine for me.

LEONIE: Ah! You really choose your time well! This is the moment when your friend—

MAXIME: Oh! My friend's reached the age of reason, madame, he knows how to act: household sulking! He wanted to give his wife a lesson; he's going to return any time soon, fresh and rosy as a school boy who played hooky; but as for me, as for me, madame, it's eleven days since I last ate! Eleven nights since I last slept!

LEONIE: Well! You must begin to make yourself do it!

MAXIME: And I am waiting for this famous delay to expire at last, which will put you in the absolute necessity of keeping your promise.

LEONIE: Me?

MAXIME: Yes, there's no longer any way to defend yourself! The eleven days have revolved; I've foreseen everything, prepared everything to leave you no escape. The banns are published, the Mayor is displaying his scarf, the church is lighting its candles, the organ is playing the prelude, and the Swiss guard is making his pike resound.

LEONIE: Ah, well, he will have to wait, the Swiss.

MAXIME: Ah! Madame, this isn't possible.

LEONIE: Why, grasp this bullheadedness?

MAXIME: Ah! Yes, grasp it, when one looks at you! And if you would listen to me.

LEONIE: But can I listen to you in the frame of mind I am in? I don't have my head about me!

MAXIME: Roquefeuille will tell you that it's an excellent frame of mind to be married in.

LEONIE: And the Panama which is waiting for me and is steaming up?

MAXIME: *(aside)* And me, too!

LEONIE: Look! Don't talk to me about anything until Robert is found.

MAXIME: And after that?

LEONIE: Ah! After that?

ROQUEFEUILLE: *(hurrying in)* Well, have you? Has he? Have they?

LEONIE: Nothing. And you?

ROQUEFEUILLE: Nothing. —And you?

MAXIME: But at Chatou?

ROQUEFEUILLE: I'm coming from there! Nothing! Nothing! Nothing!

LEONIE: This is terrifying!

ROQUEFEUILLE: It's sinister!

MAXIME: Why, you are childish with your unease! Why don't you put him in the newspaper under "Lost Articles"?

ROQUEFEUILLE: Women would run after him and not wish to return him.

LEONIE: Would you please not joke!

ROQUEFEUILLE: And Madame Maubray?

LEONIE: Ah! You judge! She will be ill over it!

ROQUEFEUILLE: Only one husband and he steals off—

LEONIE: In the midst of all this Mr. Duvernet has the heart to speak to me of marriage.

ROQUEFEUILLE: Hell! This gives him hope of getting away from you too, one day!

MAXIME: But I don't see—

LEONIE: Not another word! I will consent to forgive you only if you bring your friend back to me.

MAXIME: You are saying?

LEONIE: Begone! March! And if you bring him back—honest reward!

MAXIME: Now there's a hope that gives me wings—I have an idea.

ROQUEFEUILLE: Seize it!

MAXIME: *(looking at his watch)* Ten o'clock. The marriage is for two o'clock. I've got time. *(he escapes)*

LEONIE: Yes, yes, you've got time!

ROQUEFEUILLE: *(sitting down)* To get married! Ah! Yes, he has time. Ah! Now there's a fellow who will know the rope with which to hang himself.

LEONE: It's she! Laurence!

LAURENCE: *(entering)* Well?

LEONIE: Well! My poor Laurence, nothing new.

LAURENCE: My God!

ROQUEFEUILLE: It's not to be understood!

LAURENCE: Ah! As for me, I understand too well. He knows what we were trying to hide from him—and now he is free, he's gone, never to return!

LEONIE: Why, no! What an idea!

LAURENCE: Ah! Don't tell me no, I am sure of it! Otherwise, wouldn't he already have returned, he who was always so scrupulous to return at the agreed time, to spare me any worry? Because he was so good! He was so tender, so sweet sometimes! Ah, it's over now, it's really over, go! I've lost him and forever!

LEONIE: But I don't want you to weep like this!

LAURENCE: Now this is what comes from, wanting to trick him instead of telling him everything! Ah! If I'd told him everything!—he loves me so much!—And a few moments before his departure even—Ah! If I had known—it was so easy!

ROQUEFEUILLE: Look, look, dear lady, let's not be desolated, and let's find a remedy! You are quite sure he didn't leave the least little word of information?

LAURENCE: Not one! I've looked everywhere!

LEONIE: And since that time, not one letter, not a word to explain his behavior?

LAURENCE: No!

ROQUEFEUILLE: It's incomprehensible! And to say that this is happening to us at the moment of seriously marrying him, and riveting his chain on him! He suspected the ambush, the rogue! A plan so clever, so well executed! I foresaw everything—everything is ready, the mayor is informed, he will wait for us for two hours, after two hours it will be too late: he has an assembly of shareholders he has to preside over, and as he doesn't pay dividends, he must at least be on time! And the first marriage with which I am occupied is going to fail for the inexplicable absence of the groom! And what groom? A serious groom, tested, guaranteed! A groom passe, a posterior groom! No, no, it's not possible! He's going to come! He will come! He's coming! Here he is.

(Therese enters.)

ROQUEFEUILLE: No, this is not him!

THERESE: *(a box in her hand)* For Madame!

ROQUEFEUILLE: He can't be in there—

LAURENCE: Who is it from?

THERESE: I don't know! It was a delivery boy who told me "For Madame Maubray!"

LEONIE: Really, what can it be?

(Therese leaves.)

ROQUEFEUILLE: Will you allow me?—Ah, a jewel box!

LEONIE: A magnificent jewel box!

LAURENCE: What's it mean?

ROQUEFEUILLE: A jewel box! Ah! That's still plain enough!

LEONIE: Open it!

LEONIE, LAURENCE, AND ROQUEFEUILLE: Diamonds!

LEONIE: What a splendid necklace!

ROQUEFEUILLE: Necklace? My god it's big as a river!

LAURENCE: *(to Leonie)* Do you understand it?

LEONIE: Absolutely not!

ROQUEFEUILLE: Ah, I get it. It's a gift from friend Maxime to his fiancee!

LAURENCE: That's possible!

LEONIE: By what right does Mr. Duvernet permit himself to send me diamonds?

ROQUEFEUILLE: My word! By the right diamonds have to present themselves everywhere; anyway, at the situation you are in—

LEONIE: At the situation we are in, Mr. Duvernet is an impertinent! No, this jewel box is not for me, but for Laurence!

LAURENCE: Not at all; there's a mistake—It's for you!

ROQUEFEUILLE: Ah! It's indeed the first time I've seen two women send back a jewel!!

(Enter Baptiste hurriedly.)

BAPTISTE: Madame! Madame! Here he is!

LAURENCE: My husband?

BAPTISTE: The master! It's the master! He's getting out of a cab!

LAURENCE: Him! It's him! Ah! That makes everything all right!

ROQUEFEUILLE: We've got him! Don't let him escape! I am running to city-hall! Which way so as not to meet him?

LAURENCE: By this door!

ROQUEFEUILLE: It won't be long, the wretch! *(he leaves excitedly)*

BAPTISTE: *(announcing)* The master! *(he leaves with Therese)*

(Robert enters slowly from the back, in English traveling costume, large overcoat, cap, etc.)

LAURENCE: *(running to him and kissing him)* Ah! My friend, how happy I am to see you!

ROBERT: *(very cold, in a slightly English accent)* Very happy as well.

LEONIE: *(aside)* That tone!

LAURENCE: Ah! If you knew how worried I was by your absence!

ROBERT: No reason to be, madame.

LAURENCE: Madame! Here it is three days that you've been far from me and instead of kissing me—

ROBERT: Why didn't you say it right away! With pleasure *(kissing her coldly on the face and going to sit down)*

LAURENCE: But where are you coming from, my God?

ROBERT: I'm coming from London!

LAURENCE: From London?

LEONIE: He's frozen himself crossing the Channel!

ROBERT: Ah! Madame Vanvres, pardon me, I didn't see you. *(he bows ceremoniously)*

LEONIE: Sir!

LAURENCE: What were you doing in London, my friend?

ROBERT: Why, first of all paying a visit of politeness to my fellow citizens; because, you know, madame, that I am English, and then to correct, by living with a nation calm and cold, this petulance of character of which I gave you here even, an irritating example!

LAURENCE: Well, there, truly, I prefer you in the French way!

ROBERT: No, madame.

LAURENCE: What do you mean, no?

ROBERT: You've made me understand sufficiently that my education was not complete, and that I was lacking a certain polish.

LAURENCE: *(wanting to speak)* My God!

ROBERT: This English polish!

LEONIE: *(impatiently)* Ah, indeed, are you going to always talk like this, now?

ROBERT: *(coldly)* Always!

LAURENCE: And you will always dress like that?

ROBERT: Always!

LEONIE: And always as vibrant?

LAURENCE: As friendly?

ROBERT: Always! *(he goes to the chimney, sitting before it holding his legs in the air)*

THE TWO WOMEN: *(horrified)* Oh!

LEONIE: My dear Laurence, my sincere compliments! I see you already strolling the length of Picadilly or on the lawns of Hyde Park with a rose bonnet decorated with a green veil, a gooseberry dress, a yellow scarf on the arm of milord in a raincoat and macintosh. That's splendid! And if I weren't French, I would be English!

BAPTISTE: *(entering)* Madame!

LAURENCE: What is it this time?

BAPTISTE: A bouquet that they just brought for madame.

LEONIE: Who from?

BAPTISTE: Madame asks me—

LAURENCE: On whose behalf—?

BAPTISTE: I don't know. Here's the bouquet.

(Baptiste gives the bouquet to Laurence, enveloped in paper.)

LAURENCE: I mustn't accept.

LEONIE: A bouquet is always accepted.

(Baptiste leaves.)

LAURENCE: But, my husband?

LEONIE: *(pointing to Robert who seems to be asleep)* Does he think of you?

LAURENCE: Leonie!

LEONIE: *(pointing to Robert who is drowsing)* Here, look!

LAURENCE: *(she pulls the bouquet from its envelope and utters a scream)* Ah!

LEONIE: A bouquet of orange blossoms.

LAURENCE: Orange blossoms!

LEONIE: In any case, who is it that was able—

MAXIME: *(entering)* Arrived! Has he arrived?

LAURENCE: Yes, from England.

MAXIME: That's not possible! I'm coming from the passport office, they didn't issue one to him.

ROBERT: *(without budging from his place)* Yes! They no longer issue passports to England.

MAXIME: *(grabbing his hand)* You are breathing then! You feel well! Yes—let's go, much better!

LAURENCE: *(making him turn towards her)* Pardon! Is it you, Mr. Duvernet, who sent us these jewels?

MAXIME: What jewels?

LEONIE: Is it you, Mr. Duvernet who sent us this bouquet?

MAXIME: What jewels? What bouquet?

LAURENCE: *(pointing to the jewel box)* This one!

LEONIE: *(showing him the bouquet)* This one!

MAXIME: These diamonds! These flowers!

LEONIE: Perhaps you haven't noticed what sort of flowers?

MAXIME: Orange buds! *(laughing)* Ah! Ha!

LAURENCE: You are laughing?

MAXIME: I don't know who sent you this bouquet, but I swear it wasn't me.

LEONIE: Then who can it be?

ROQUEFEUILLE: *(entering rapidly and announcing)* It's me!

LEONIE: What do you mean it's you?

ROQUEFEUILLE: Eh! By Jove! Yes, it's me! Is Robert ready?

LAURENCE: Ah! You are the author of such mystification?

ROQUEFEUILLE: What mystification?

LEONIE: I ought to have suspected it

ROQUEFEUILLE: *(speechless)* But what? *(Leonie shows him the bouquet)*

LEONIE: You have the impertinence to send a bouquet of orange blossoms to me, Madame de Vanvres?

ROQUEFEUILLE: Orange blossoms! To you, again! Thanks! What a joke! I might have understood a carton of oranges!

LEONIE: Then it wasn't you?

MAXIME: No, I swear.

LAURENCE: *(to Roquefeuille)* Nor you?

ROQUEFEUILLE: Why, by Jove! Let's move on! Where is Robert?

LAURENCE AND LEONIE: Hush!

ROQUEFEUILLE: God forgive me! I think he's sleeping!

LEONIE: He's really got the look of it!

ROQUEFEUILLE: He really picked his time well! I've just come from city hall, we don't have a minute to lose. Wake him up, wake him up! He cannot appear in that outfit before the authorities!

LAURENCE: Why, why not?

ROQUEFEUILLE: *(exasperated)* Eh! It's your affair, by Jove! Since this morning, I've only gone up and down stairs, and run from the church to the city hall and the city hall to the church! The mayor sent me to his vicar, and the assistant who sent me to his beadle. And the cabs and the coachmen and the crowd of brats! Mr. Mayor!—Mr. Mayor! Yes, yes, I'm making fun of you. The Mayor. Try to understand me! Go!

MAXIME: Why then, why then! Madame consents. You are consenting then?

LEONIE: Huh?

MAXIME: Why this marriage! This church, this city hall! It's for us!

LEONIE: For us!

MAXIME: Damn!

ROQUEFEUILLE: Heavens, it's true, he knows nothing about it! Let's leave him in his error! The unfortunate!

MAXIME: *(to Leonie)* Ah! Madame! If you consent—a word, a single word!

ROQUEFEUILLE: *(making Leonie move)* Go get dressed!

MAXIME: As a bride?

LEONIE: Not at all, sir, as a bridesmaid!

ROQUEFEUILLE: Then keep the bouquet so the illusion will be complete!

(Leonie shrugs her shoulders.)

LEONIE: Ah! You are an impertinent! *(she leaves)*

MAXIME: But I don't understand a thing! But if it's not me who is getting married, who's getting married here?

ROQUEFEUILLE: That doesn't concern you. *(to Laurence)* Hurry up, I'm going to keep the mayor patient. *(Pointing to Robert)* Dress him! *(to Maxime)* Come on, march!

LAURENCE: But my friend—

ROQUEFEUILLE: Black tie—it's de riguer! A marriage, grand mourning. *(He drags Maxime off)*

LAURENCE: An hour! I have only an hour and Robert's sleeping. How to get him out of this costume to put a black suit on?

(She approaches him and calls him softly) Robert, my friend, Robert. *(he snores a bit)* Oh! *(calling anew)* Robert!

ROBERT: Ah! I think by Jove! That I was sleeping! What a rude character I am!

LAURENCE: It's not a great evil, my friend, especially if you are worn out!

ROBERT: That's my excuse if I may invoke one!

LAURENCE: Do you need something?

ROBERT: I need my bed. *(stretches out on the sofa)*

LAURENCE: His bed! *(aloud)* Don't you think it would be better to get out of these heavy clothes?

ROBERT: I would, willingly enough, but I will confess to you that I feel myself so at ease in this excellent little sofa that the least movement terrifies me!

LAURENCE: That doesn't matter! Am I not here?

ROBERT: I don't wish to abuse.

LAURENCE: On the contrary, it's a pleasure for me. Between young marrieds, these little efforts, aren't they a proof of tenderness that one loves to give?

ROBERT: *(incredulous)* Oh! Oh!

LAURENCE: You doubt it? Isn't your wife your housekeeper?

ROBERT: What you are saying is very nice, my dear Laurence, and I pay you my sincere compliment, if you still see life still lit in the reflections of our honey moon! But—

LAURENCE: But—?

ROBERT: You are behindhand! The years are slipping by, and what used to appear as a charming game and full of poetry, risks today becoming ridiculous nonsense.

LAURENCE: Am I hearing you?

ROBERT: I astonish you?

LAURENCE: Why, yes, I confess it. And what you are tell me, it's barely three years—*(She sits on the cassock near Robert)*

ROBERT: *(rising abruptly)* Pardon me!

LAURENCE: Ah—you are leaving me!

ROBERT: No—but if someone surprised us they would perhaps think we were amorous.

LAURENCE: What of it, my friend?

ROBERT: What of it—that would be a little ridiculous!

LAURENCE: Ridiculous! That you love your wife and that your wife loves you?

ROBERT: Did I say that? In that case, I was expressing myself badly.

LAURENCE: *(reanimated)* Ah!

ROBERT: I love you, my dear Laurence, I love you reasonably and seriously, as one must love one's wife, after three years of marriage.

LAURENCE: Meaning love can't resist three years of marriage, right?

ROBERT: That depends on the regime to which it is submitted, my dear! It closely resembles water that you place on fire. The more hot the fire, the quicker the water becomes steam! Thus, with love—

LAURENCE: Are we there?

ROBERT: Not yet!

LAURENCE: Not yet is full of promises.

ROBERT: But it's the fate which awaits a man crazy enough to believe in eternal youth; let's not struggle and obey the laws of nature.

LAURENCE: That's charming! Meaning—

ROBERT: Meaning that in the autumn of life, one mustn't ask for the poetry of spring nor the ardors of summer.

LAURENCE: *(troubled)* Ah! Robert, how can you say that to me?

ROBERT: What you made me understand, although you didn't say it to me, three days ago! I thought it over and I saw how wise you were.

LAURENCE: No indeed!

ROBERT: *(laughing)* Yes, indeed!

LAURENCE: Are you sure of having clearly understood?

ROBERT: Perfectly! Decidedly, you were right! These clothes are heavy! So, I'm going to follow your opinion and change 'em! *(goes into his room)*

LAURENCE: *(alone)* He no longer loves me! I no longer suspect it now! You don't talk like this if you are in love. He no longer loves me.

ROQUEFEUILLE: *(entering)* Are you ready?

LAURENCE: Not yet!

ROQUEFEUILLE: Let's not joke; the cabs are following me. I am in a sweat.

LAURENCE: Robert went into his room; he's going to find his clothes prepared on his bed, with his gloves and his white tie. I hid the other clothes.

ROQUEFEUILLE: Good, good! Still a half hour! You know—the mayor—his shareholders. No dividends! He must be on time! I am going to keep him patient, he will make me patient, we will make each other patient. But by Jove if they ever catch me marrying someone!

LAURENCE: Marry us! Ah, no my friend! Robert's not going to want to marry anymore; he no longer loves me!

ROQUEFEUILLE: What?

LAURENCE: Once at city-hall, he's going to say, "No"!

ROQUEFEUILLE: Not bluntly like that?

LAURENCE: I would never have thought it. But it's a horrible fear which is coming to me suddenly!

ROQUEFEUILLE: *(terrified)* Why, no! No indeed! What an idea! Now there's an idea for goodness sake!

LAURENCE: Hush! He's coming!

ROQUEFEUILLE: You see clearly, he has his black gloves, his white suit—that is to say—no. Anyway, little matters, he's dressed, we are saved.

ROBERT: *(entering in slippers and robe)* There!

ROQUEFEUILLE AND LAURENCE: Ah!

ROBERT: The fact is I'm more comfortable this way!

LAURENCE: *(stupefied)* In a bath robe?

ROBERT: Yes, in a bath robe!

ROQUEFEUILLE: In slippers?

ROBERT: And in slippers. Heavens, you here? Hello, I really had enough trouble finding them.

LAURENCE: But, my friend, it's impossible for you to remain like this!

ROQUEFEUILLE: It's impractical!

ROBERT: Impractical, why?

LAURENCE: Why, if someone comes to visit?

ROQUEFEUILLE: Yes, —several visits—a herd of visits.

ROBERT: I will lock the door.

LAURENCE: You are going to suffocate!

ROQUEFEUILLE: He's going to suffocate! It's so hot—

ROBERT: I will open the window!

LAURENCE: That's impossible.

ROQUEFEUILLE: Impossible! It's so cold.

ROBERT: *(drily)* Impossible! I don't understand, my dear Laurence, you engage me to leave my traveling clothes for me to rest, I listen to you, I slip into my bathrobe, I slip on my slippers, and you are not satisfied? Truly, what do you want? For me to put on a white tie and black suit?

ROQUEFEUILLE: Why, exactly—there it is—that's what we want!

ROBERT: You will never persuade me that this is dress for the master of the house. Then, put on a fancy dress and light the lights!

LAURENCE: *(aside)* What to do, my God!

ROQUEFEUILLE: *(to Laurence)* And the mayor who's waiting on pins and needles! You've got to reveal—

LAURENCE: Never! That would be risking everything!

ROBERT: Why, what's the matter with you?

LAURENCE: Me, I—

ROQUEFEUILLE: Oh! An idea!—By Jove, yes!

ROBERT: Well?

ROQUEFEUILLE: Well, yes, my friend, I've lost.

ROBERT: Lost? Lost what?

ROQUEFEUILLE: A wager that I made with these ladies, and that you've made me lose!

ROBERT: Explain yourself!

ROQUEFEUILLE: You've half guessed it. I wanted to make you leave your traveling clothes, not for a bath robe, but for a black formal. I bet with these ladies to get to that result without letting you know, I lost!

ROBERT: You see! And what was the reason for this masquerade?

ROQUEFEUILLE: They'll tell you when you are disguised.

ROBERT: No, before, or I won't disguise myself!

ROQUEFEUILLE: What bullheadedness! Before, so be it! You are the witness to your friend Maxime, who's getting married in a half-hour at the city-hall of the quarter.

LAURENCE: *(low)* For goodness sake!

ROQUEFEUILLE: Hush! It was the only way. *(low)*

ROBERT: He's getting married?

ROQUEFEUILLE: He's getting married. Ah! I think so indeed, the character! Everybody gets married, she's getting married.

LAURENCE: *(still hesitant)* But—

ROBERT: Madame de Vanvres has agreed with—

ROQUEFEUILLE: No, without enthusiasm!

ROBERT: And it's in a half hour?

ROQUEFEUILLE: In a half hour!

LAURENCE: *(low)* My God! You—

ROQUEFEUILLE: *(low)* I told you it's the only way!

ROBERT: Why didn't you tell me sooner, my dear?

LAURENCE: Me! Tell you that—

ROQUEFEUILLE: And the bet?

ROBERT: The bet, that's right! Let's go! So much the better! There's our friend Maxime, the happiest of men!

ROQUEFEUILLE: After you!

ROBERT: After me?

ROQUEFEUILLE: Come on, quick! This outfit, this tie—

ROBERT: Black, right?

ROQUEFEUILLE: White! Wretch.

ROBERT: Do you think a long tie—

ROQUEFEUILLE: White! White! White! A witness is almost a husband!

ROBERT: Don't worry! In five minutes you will have an irreproachable witness! *(goes into his room)*

ROQUEFEUILLE: It's done! *(falling into a chair)*

LAURENCE: But what are you thinking of? To tell him that Leonie is going to get married?

ROQUEFEUILLE: That was the only means I had.

LAURENCE: But she doesn't want to.

ROQUEFEUILLE: It's necessary that she want to.

LAURENCE: But think—

ROQUEFEUILLE: I am not thinking, I am not thinking! Since this morning I haven't known what I am doing—and you plainly see, because I've just married someone—me!

LAURENCE: But—

ROQUEFEUILLE: Don't say but. You've driven me mad with your marriage. And, since it is like that, well, yes! I will drag Madame de Vanvres to the altar, I will drag Robert to the altar, and I will drag myself, where we will tell everybody why—

LAURENCE: There's not a moment to lose! Got to warn Leonie at least!

ROQUEFEUILLE: Warn her, don't warn her, it's all the same to me! I am running to the church to make the Swiss patient!

LAURENCE: One moment!

ROQUEFEUILLE: *(without listening to her)* I suspect the Swiss! *(Leonie enters)* Ah! Madame de Vanvres! Victory! He's dressing like a groom! Now this is still the most beautiful day of life! By Jove! In that case what is the most ugly? *(He leaves)*

LEONIE: He's dressing as a groom?

LAURENCE: Not positively!

LEONIE: What do you mean!

LAURENCE: But it's the same outfit.

LEONIE: The same costume?

LAURENCE: My dear Leonie! My only, my unique friend! My fate is in your hands!

LEONIE: Speak!

LAURENCE: Then learn—

(Robert enters in full attire.)

ROBERT: *(bowing)* Madame!

LAURENCE: *(aside)* For now, it's over.

ROBERT: *(to Leonie)* You see I haven't kept any rancor for your misdeeds towards me?

LEONIE: I see it—in what?

ROBERT: You haven't noticed this dignified and solemn attire?

LEONIE: In what way, I beg you, is this dignified and solemn attire a proof that you have forgotten my misdeeds?

LAURENCE: *(to Leonie)* Shut up!

LEONIE: *(astonished)* Huh?

ROBERT: What! You are still jesting at this supreme moment?

LEONIE: What supreme moment?

ROBERT: Why is there nothing sacred for you about it?

LEONIE: What isn't sacred?

ROBERT: Ah! For goodness sake, that's too much. If this is the way you reward your witnesses?

LEONIE: What witness?

LAURENCE: *(low)* Silence! Wretched woman! I didn't have the time to tell you that you are getting married in ten minutes.

LEONIE: *(speechless)* Me?

MAXIME: *(entering)* Ah! Robert in black suit!

ROBERT: Yes, my dear friend, on your account.

MAXIME: On my account?

ROBERT: Are we going to start all over? Word of honor, they are crazy.

LEONIE: *(low to Laurence)* This passes all bounds, and it a strange abuse—

LAURENCE: Listen to me.

ROBERT: I am the witness for Madame de Vanvres, who you are marrying in ten minutes.

MAXIME: You are saying that—?

ROBERT: Happiness has put your head topsy-turvy.

MAXIME: *(to Leonie)* Ah! You consent, madame! Joy, shock—

LEONIE: Excuse me, excuse me—

LAURENCE: Leonie!

MAXIME: Madame!

ROBERT: What, still hesitations? When you are perfectly decided, you can inform me. *(goes into his room)*

LEONIE: *(to Laurence)* Why, you know you are putting me in a frightful position!

LAURENCE: It was the only way to make him put on a black suit!

MAXIME: *(astonished)* My marriage depends on Robert's black suit?

LEONIE: Here I am handsomely compromised.

MAXIME: One word, madame and I will return you the honor!

LEONIE: Leave me alone! This is really about you!

LAURENCE: It was necessary! By seeing you consent to your marriage, he will be forced to consent to his.

MAXIME: Who's he?

LEONIE: This doesn't concern you! Listen, Laurence, I consent to a compromise, I will accompany you to city-hall, but don't ask anything more of me!

LAURENCE: That's not enough!

MAXIME: *(repeating without understanding)* That's not enough!

LAURENCE: If you say no, he will say no, too.

MAXIME: *(stupefied)* He will say no, too!

ROQUEFEUILLE: *(entering)* Let's go! Let's go! The mayor's impatient, and the Swiss wouldn't listen.

LEONIE: I absolutely must marry Mr. Duvernet!

ROQUEFEUILLE: Two marriages! Very fine. The more fools there are, the more they laugh. Forward march!

MAXIME: Ah, indeed! But whose is the second marriage? Is it yours?

ROQUEFEUILLE: No bad jokes!

MAXIME: Still!

ROQUEFEUILLE: None of your business. Let's go! Move!

LAURENCE: My dear Leonie!

MAXIME: Madame!

LEONIE: Well?

LAURENCE: Well?

ROQUEFEUILLE: Come on, then! What are you doing there?

LEONIE: *(giving Maxime her hand)* It's not for you, anyway, sir!

ROQUEFEUILLE: There's one—now the other!

LAURENCE: Call Robert!

ROQUEFEUILLE: Robert! Robert!

LEONIE: Could he have taken flight?

ROQUEFEUILLE: I don't have time to wait for him, I am running to the city-hall; all you've got is a few minutes! En route! *(he leaves)*

LEONIE: Let's go my dear, sir, is happiness paralyzing you? Find this unfindable Robert for us!

MAXIME: *(leaving)* Robert! Robert!

LAURENCE: *(kissing Leonie)* Ah! It's to you that I owe my happiness!

LEONIE: I hope I'll be able to say as much?

LAURENCE: He loves you! He will make you happy!

LEONIE: May God wish it!

LAURENCE: But Robert! Where is Robert? *(she leaves—Baptiste and Therese enter)* Have you seen my husband?

THERESE: Why, madame—

LAURENCE: At the last moment! Run! Look!

(Maxime enters.)

LEONIE: Well?

MAXIME: Nobody!

LEONIE: Nobody!

LAURENCE: It's fate!

LEONIE: Two o'clock is going to strike!

MAXIME: Robert!

LAURENCE: Robert!

LEONIE: Mr. Maubray!

BAPTISTE AND THERESE: Sir! Sir!

ROBERT: *(entering)* Somebody call me?

MAXIME: We've got him.

LAURENCE: At last!

LEONIE: Quick, give me your arm and let's get going!

ROBERT: Here it is!

(Two o'clock strikes.)

LEONIE: Two o'clock!

ALL: Two o'clock

ROQUEFEUILLE: *(entering, breathless)* Too late!

LAURENCE: It's all over. *(she collapses on the sofa)*

ROQUEFEUILLE: The mayor left in a rage. He won't come back!

MAXIME: And to think I had reached port! *(collapsing in an armchair)*

LEONIE: Poor Laurence!

(Moment of silence and embarrassment.)

ROBERT: *(pulling white gloves out of his pocket, slowly putting them on, approaching Laurence)* Miss?

ALL: Huh?

ROBERT: Will Miss Laurence de Croix do me the honor of granting me her hand?

LAURENCE: *(rising)* Robert—then you knew?

ROBERT: Everything!

LAURENCE: Ah! How I love you! *(she falls in his arms)*

ROQUEFEUILLE: Bravo! Well played!

MAXIME: If I understand any of this—

LAURENCE: My dear husband—

ROBERT: *(smiling)* Not yet—

LEONIE: But how did you guess—

ROQUEFEUILLE: Yes, how—?

ROBERT: *(pulling the newspaper from his pocket)* This paper that you tried to hide from me, and that Baptiste unearthed for me three days ago, put me on the trail, and the clerk at city-hall to whom Roquefeuille had to reveal everything, informed me of the rest!

ROQUEFEUILLE: And you wanted to take your revenge?

ROBERT: On your mysteries and your secrets!

MAXIME: What mysteries? What secrets?

LAURENCE: So this departure?

ROBERT: Comedy!

LAURENCE: This coldness?

ROBERT: That especially was comedy! Eh, what! Little crazy-head, you doubted me for a single moment? You were able to believe that I no longer loved you?

LAURENCE: Forgive!

ROQUEFEUILLE: Very fine! Very fine! But with all that, the Mayor—

ROBERT: I was the meeting of shareholders! The mayor is waiting for us!

ROQUEFEUILLE: Still! *(to Maxime)* Go collect your dividends! *(leading him to Madame de Vanvres)*

MAXIME: Let's hope that one day they will explain this to me.

ROQUEFEUILLE: What for, since, as in all comedies it ends in a marriage.

ROBERT: With two marriages.

MAXIME: *(taking Leonie's hand)* Mine and?

ROBERT: *(taking Laurence's hand)* And mine!

MAXIME: Ah, bah!

ROQUEFEUILLE: Your example profits me—I will do the same— if it's possible to marry—without taking a wife.

CURTAIN

Contributors

JEAN-MICHEL MARGOT is an internationally recognized specialist on Jules Verne. He currently serves as president of the North American Jules Verne Society and has published several books and many articles on the author. Margot edited Verne's theatrical play *Journey Through the Impossible* (Prometheus, 2003), a volume of the 19th century Verne criticism, *Jules Verne en son temps* (Encrage, 2004), and provided the introduction and notes of Verne's *The Kip Brothers* (Wesleyan University Press, 2007).

FRANK MORLOCK, Public Health Service Officer (LtCMDR, Retd.), was born in Boston in 1941. Attending Boston University and Boston University Law School, he was always interested in writing for theatre. Two hundred plays are now on the internet (on such sites as Project Gutenberg, Blackmask.com, the Alexandre Dumas web page, and the Napoleonic Literature page), about two-thirds of which are adaptations, and the remainder translations. Four plays have been published by Rogue, who put out an ebook version of his translation of the stage version of Verne's *Around the World in Eighty Days*. In 2006 he was honored by the North American Jules Verne Society, and Morlock's translations of Verne's plays *Michael Strogoff*, *The Children of Captain Grant*, *The Voyage Through the Impossible*, and *Mathias Sandorf* have all been published through Borgo-Wildside Press. He has also penned a number of original dramas of his own, and currently lives and works in Mexico.

BRIAN TAVES (Ph.D., University of Southern California) has been an archivist in the Motion Picture, Broadcasting, and Recorded Sound Division of the Library of Congress since 1990. He is the author of over 100 articles and 25 chapters in anthologies. Taves has also written books on P.G. Wodehouse and Hollywood; director Robert Florey; the genre of historical adventure movies; and fantasy-adventure writer Talbot Mundy, in addition to editing an original anthology of Mundy's best stories. In 2002-2003, Taves was chosen as Kluge Staff Fellow at the Library to write the first book on silent film pioneer Thomas Ince, to appear in 2011. Taves's writing on Verne has been translated into French, German, and Spanish, and he is currently writing a book on the 300 film and television adaptations of Verne worldwide. Taves is coauthor of *The Jules Verne Encyclopedia* (Scarecrow, 1996), and edited the first English-language publication of Verne's *Adventures of the Rat Family* (Oxford, 1993).

Acknowledgements

The Society also appreciates the efforts of members who have contributed to this volume, including Dennis Kytasaari and Noel Gibilaro, as well as such friends as Jean Frodsham, Elvira Berkowitsch, Pachara Yongvongpaibul, and David March of the Rafael Sabatini Society.

The Palik series, while spearheaded by the North American Jules Verne Society, represents a cooperative effort among Vernians worldwide, pooling the resources and knowledge of the various organizations in different countries. We are grateful for the assistance of Philippe Burgaud and J.A. Marquis for this volume.

Internationally renowned Verne expert **Volker Dehs** provided a close reading and always-helpful suggestions, offering rare illustrations from his personal collection.

The Society is grateful for research assistance from Frédéric Jaccaud, curator of Jean-Michel Margot's Verne Collection at the Maison d'Ailleurs (House of Elsewhere) in Yverdon-les-Bains, Switzerland.

We are particularly indebted to **Bernhard Krauth,** chairman of the German Jules-Verne-Club since 2005. A deep sea licensed master working today as a docking pilot in Bremerhaven, Germany, Bernhard has published several Verne-related articles in France, the Netherlands and Germany. Intensely interested in the illustrations of the original French editions of Verne's work, he has been deeply involved in a project to digitize the illustrations, more than 5,000 in all. The project is for common, non-commercial use, and most of the illustrations in this publication were made possible through his generosity.

❧

The Palik Series

The last two decades have brought astonishing progress in the study of Jules Verne, with many new translations of Verne stories, including the discovery of many texts. Still, there remain a number of Verne stories that have been overlooked, and it is this gap that the North American Jules Verne Society seeks to fill in the Palik series.

Through the generosity of our late member, Edward Palik, and the pooling of expertise by a variety of Verne scholars and translators around the world, we will be able to bring to the Anglophone public a series of hitherto unknown Verne tales.

Ed Palik had a special enthusiasm for bringing neglected Verne stories to English-speaking readers, and this will be reflected in the series that bears his name. In this way the society hopes to fulfill the goal that Ed's consideration has made possible. The volumes published will reveal the amazing range of Verne's storytelling, in genres that may surprise those who only know his most famous stories. We hope to allow a better appreciation of the famous writer who has, for more than a century and a half, been the widest-read author of fiction in the world.

CPSIA information can be obtained at www.ICGtesting.com

263726BV00005B/93/P

9 781593 933630